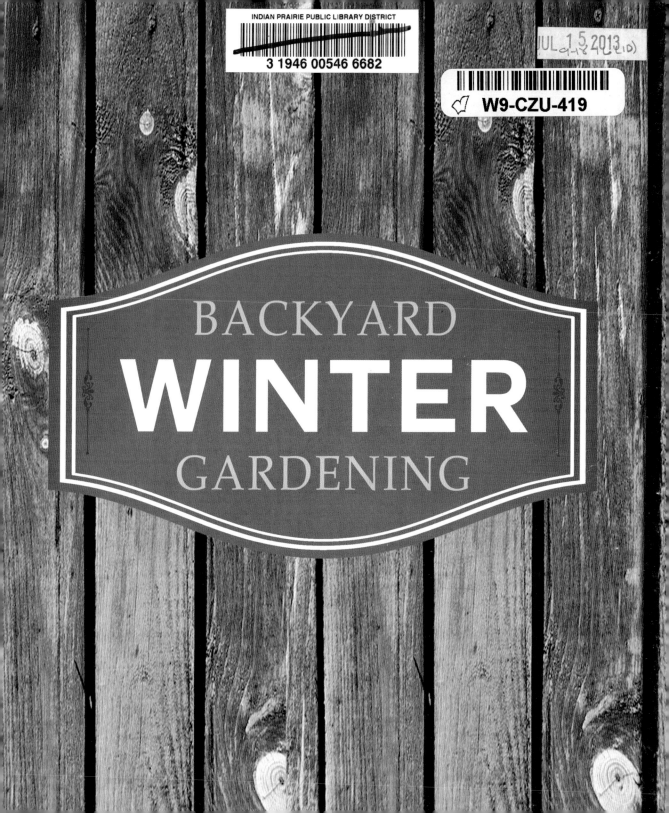

BACKYARD
WINTER
GARDENING

BACKYARD
WINTER
GARDENING

VEGETABLES FRESH AND SIMPLE, IN ANY CLIMATE, WITHOUT ARTIFICIAL HEAT OR ELECTRICITY—THE WAY IT'S BEEN DONE FOR 2,000 YEARS

BESTSELLING AUTHOR OF
*THE FORGOTTEN SKILLS OF
SELF-SUFFICIENCY USED BY THE
MORMON PIONEERS*

*& THE ART OF BAKING WTH
NATURAL YEAST*

CALEB WARNOCK

HOBBLE CREEK PRESS | SPRINGVILLE, UTAH

ISBN 13: 978-1-4621-1094-0

Published by Hobble Creek Press, an imprint of Cedar Fort, Inc.

2373 W. 700 S., Springville, UT, 84663

Distributed by Cedar Fort, Inc., www.cedarfort.com

LIBRARY OF CONGRESS CATALOGING-IN-PUBLICATION DATA

Warnock, Caleb (Caleb J.), 1973- author.
 Backyard winter gardening : vegetables fresh and simple, in any climate, without artificial heat or electricity, the way it's been done for 2,000 years / Caleb Warnock.
    pages cm
 Includes bibliographical references and index.
 ISBN 978-1-4621-1094-0 (alk. paper)
 1. Vegetable gardening--Great Basin. 2. Vegetables--Great Basin. I. Title.

 SB321.5.G74W37 2013
 635.0941--dc23

                        2012042721

Cover and page design by Erica Dixon

Cover design © 2013 by Lyle Mortimer

Edited and typeset by Casey J. Winters

Printed in China

10 9 8 7 6 5 4 3 2 1

DEDICATION

TO MY WIFE, CHARMAYNE, who often says that when we met, I was a gardener in need of a garden, and she had a garden in need of a gardener. We transplanted raspberries on one of our first dates, and for ten years we've been growing beautiful things together. I love you better than the fresh raspberries I picked out of our backyard this afternoon during the surprise summer rain! These past ten years with you and the kids have been my joy.

I DEDICATE THIS BOOK TO MY LAST LIVING GRANDPARENT, Grandma "Billie" Nielson. What would I be today without your home, your farm, your cooking, your garden, and years of wisdom from you and Grandpa? I found myself a surprise grandpa at a young age, and I could not have done it without your years of daily example. I strive to be the same kind of grandparent to my grandchildren that you are to me. Every day of my childhood, a plaque hung on your kitchen wall that read, "Everything Cometh to He who Waiteth, so Long as He who Waiteth, Worketh like Hell while He Waiteth." I have tried to live this motto in my garden and everywhere else. Thank you for teaching me.

CONTENTS

Contents

ix

Contents

PREFACE
A Fresh Winter Vegetable Buffet

"The Parisian growers . . . for generations past have practised the art of raising vegetables and salads to perfection during the worst months of the year" (Weathers, French Market-Gardening, 1909, v).

A thick January snow has been falling outside for hours, slowly whiting out the yard and garden. Our leafless apricot tree stands as a frosty work of art, and the long branches of the mugo pine bend toward the earth, burdened by snow. I have fed extra food to our horse, two cows, and thirty-five chickens, and they are content and settled for the night. The vegetable garden is at the mercy of the winter night wind.

Today, most people would assume my vegetable beds underneath the January snow are sleeping, lying dormant until spring brings back life, growth, and fresh food.

Not so.

Alerted to the coming storm by the weather forecast, I have been busy in the garden for days, picking lettuce and globe onions, watering the peas, cutting leaves of Swiss chard, and pulling up rutabaga. I have planted hundreds of seeds in the January garden soil—cantaloupe, peas, gourmet lettuces, cucumbers, onions, collards, mustard greens, herbs.

At our house, we eat fresh produce from our garden every day of the year, no matter the weather or the season. This is not a research book—this is the way we live every day. Every photo in this book was taken in our backyard garden. Our way of life is not an experiment—this is the way families have eaten for centuries. Before the invention of 24-hour grocery stores, industrial food, and groceries shipped from around the world, families fed themselves in winter by picking fresh fruit and vegetables from their backyard winter garden.

In our backyard right now, beneath five inches of white-powder snow, you will find at least four varieties of fresh, tall green lettuce, along with tender Chinese cabbage, crinkly spinach, onions, peas, strawberry plants, rutabaga, Swiss chard, mustard greens, potatoes, kale, carrots, and beets. Even fresh tomatoes off the vine (with a little extra investment). And not just a few vegetables—enough good vegetables to feed our family, day after day.

Enough to feed a crowd, in fact. One recent weekend, I was asked to teach a class on winter gardening. I decided that if a picture is worth a thousand words, then a fresh winter vegetable buffet must be better. So just before the class started, I went out into the blowing snow and picked some fresh vegetables, brought them to class, and fed the forty truly easy ways to feast straight from a fresh backyard garden in the dead of winter. I live in the Rocky Mountain West, and my coldest backyard temperature has been seventeen below zero. So if I can enjoy fresh garden salad in January, so can you! No greenhouse required—no artificial heating of any kind, no artificial lighting, no elec-

THE GOOD NEWS IS THAT FEEDING YOUR FAMILY FRESH FOOD FROM YOUR OWN BACKYARD GARDEN ALL WINTER LONG IS LESS WORK, FAR EASIER, AND LESS TIME-CONSUMING THAN YOU MIGHT IMAGINE.

people waiting for me. I think it's fair to say that most of the people in attendance were surprised, shocked, gobsmacked. I think this is fair to say because they said so themselves.

I only mention this to make a comparison. Without fresh, all-natural winter gardening, the people of Paris, London, and New York City would have starved to death in the seventeenth, eighteenth, and nineteenth centuries. Not too many generations ago, my ancestors—and yours—would have been shocked to learn that their future generations would have all but completely lost the know-how necessary to feed themselves and their livestock fresh garden food in winter without relying on someone else. To our ancestors, that notion would have been ludicrous or alarming, or both.

This book is about being useful and educational, about helping families relearn the

tricity. Learn which vegetable varieties can stay unprotected in the backyard garden all winter, even at seventeen below zero. Learn the forgotten skill of growing "nocturnal" or "sleeping" vegetables and how to use the two-thousand-year-old art of growing fresh winter food under cold frames and in simple, all-natural hotbeds.

xiii

Learn dozens of winter vegetable varieties you can grow this winter, including carrots, lettuce, spinach, peas, chard, and much more. This book explains how to grow them, and where to find the now-rare seeds. Everyone can do something to feed their family, no matter your schedule or where you live—a huge farm, a couple of acres, a condo, or a rented apartment. I have lived in all of these, and I have grown my own food in all of these places to some degree. If you want to do it, you can. You may not do everything in this book this winter, but you can do something. In today's uncertain economy, it's time to be self-sufficient.

The good news is that feeding your family fresh food from your own backyard garden all winter long is less work, far easier, and less time-consuming than you might imagine. And you won't find better tasting food at any price!

(I should note that our family eats out of the cellar all winter too, but this book does not address cellaring vegetables in detail. For more in-depth information about cellaring, please refer to my first book, *The Forgotten Skills of Self-Sufficiency Used by the Mormon Pioneers*.)

CALEB WARNOCK
January 24, 2012
Utah County, Utah

xiv

ACKNOWLEDGMENTS

I am full of gratitude to my family, without whom this book would not exist.

I am lucky enough to remember exploring and eating out of the vast gardens and cellars of both my maternal and paternal great-grandparents, in Lynndyl, Utah, and Sigurd, Utah.

My grandparents on both sides took me into their gardens for years, and I marveled over the wonderful things we could harvest and eat together. All of those gardens are now gone, but their years of teaching live on in me, and now in my grandson, Xander, who loves to garden too. Much love to Grandma and Grandpa Warnock and Grandma and Grandpa Nielson.

My own parents let me garden in our backyard when I wanted and let me make a raised strawberry bed, which was the pride of my childhood. I wandered Lynndyl and Leamington, Utah, digging tulips from abandoned pioneer-era homes and wildflowers from the countryside, planting them in our yard. Thank you, Mom and Dad, for bringing us up in these towns. I will never forget the day you took us to that house in the Salt Lake Valley and announced we were moving. But when it came time, Ashley and I cried for so long, so hard, that you changed your mind. How grateful I am. What a wonderful place to grow up, in the Utah desert

on our farm. Thank you, Mom and Dad, for your years of sacrifice.

Thank you, Phronsie and John, for letting Xander and Ada grow up in our garden. My happiest, most meaningful moments in the garden have been with them. (I'll never forget the day I came outside to find Xander giving my garden tour, almost word for word, to one of his little friends. He's been listening! And he was so sincere in showing each of the plants. It touched my heart. I love you, Xander.)

To all my writing teachers, my writing students, and my writing critique groups over the years—buckets of love. I wouldn't be doing this without all of your support. No man has a better group of friends and supporters than I do.

To the whole team at Cedar Fort Publishing. Thank you for believing in my books. What a ride!

Finally, to the tens of thousands of people who have toured our garden, taken my classes, invited me to give speeches and demonstrations, traded seed with me, read my blogs, and purchased my books—I had you in mind as I wrote every page of this book. My only goal has been to write a useful book for you.

xv

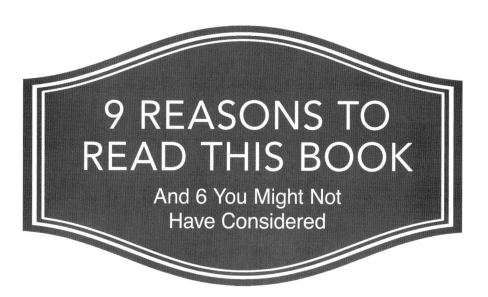

9 REASONS TO READ THIS BOOK

And 6 You Might Not Have Considered

1 Food Security for Your Family

You can feed your family fresh garden produce from your backyard twelve months a year without electricity. This book will teach you how. This food security is financial—you won't have to give your money to a grocery store. This security is also about health; for the first time, you will be able to control what chemicals are used, or not used, on your food. Speaking of chemicals, think about this:

Why don't grocery store potatoes sprout and then rot?

If you have ever grown a potato in your backyard garden, you know for sure that if you put your own backyard potatoes on the display in the grocery store next to their potatoes, your garden potatoes—because they are not stored in a cold, dark place—would immediately erupt in huge, long sprouts. Sprouting would soon turn them soft, and they would begin to rot.

If our homegrown potatoes sprout in light or warmth, why are the potatoes in the grocery store not sprouting the same giant sprouts? (Okay, some grocery store potatoes do sometimes send out pathetic sprouts when they are old, but nothing like real garden potato sprouts if you've ever seen them).

The answer to why grocery store potatoes don't sprout and then rot is two-fold. First, grocery store potatoes are treated with a chemical called "Chlorpropham," often sold under the names Bud Nip, Sprout Nip, Beet-Kleen, and Taterpex.

Second, the potatoes are exposed to so-called "low level" nuclear radiation. This is called irradiation.

These two answers lead to more questions. First, did you know your grocery store potatoes were treated with a chemical, or radiation, or both? Not likely, because by federal law, potato sellers are not required to reveal

Is the Chemical Safe?

A 1993 STUDY SAYS THIS:

"Chlorpropham is moderately toxic by ingestion. It may cause irritation of the eyes or skin. Symptoms of poisoning in laboratory animals have included listlessness, incoordination, nose bleeds, protruding eyes, bloody tears, difficulty in breathing, prostration, inability to urinate, high fevers, and death. Autopsies of animals have shown inflammation of the stomach and intestinal lining, congestion of the brain, lungs and other organs, and degenerative changes in the kidneys and liver.

". . . Chronic exposure of laboratory animals has caused retarded growth, increased liver, kidney and spleen weights, congestion of the spleen and death."

(Cornell University, "Chlorpropham")

this information. You read that right: potato growers and sellers can legally, under federal law, keep silent about the fact that the potatoes are treated with a chemical, or radiation, or both.

When you buy treated potatoes in the grocery store, you can't see the chemicals, and you don't know what the chemicals are. Cauliflower, for example, doesn't come with a warning label listing the chemicals that have been sprayed on it. But chemicals *have* been sprayed on it.

Not being able to see those chemicals, either on the vegetables or on a label, makes it easy to dismiss the chemicals. When you raise your food at home, there is a real clarity about chemicals—you know that what you put on your vegetable garden you will later put in your mouth. You suddenly begin

to wonder why you are spending money on these expensive chemicals and what the health impacts may be. Didn't people grow these same vegetables for centuries without spending money on these chemicals? The truth is, those chemicals exist only because people are making money on them. These nonsense chemicals hadn't even been invented as families fed themselves in the past—so why use them now?

Weak Vegetables

Many tests and studies have confirmed that the nutrients in food from the grocery store have been slowly dropping, but few people know why. The answer is irradiation. Industrial food producers expose the fruits, vegetables, and meat they sell to low levels of radiation as a method of killing pathogens. They say they do this to increase quality, which is ironic because they also admit the practice actually dramatically decreases the nutrients in the food when the nutrients are damaged and destroyed by the radiation.

If you think about it a moment, you realize that you get food that has been exposed to radiation, which has destroyed some of the nutrition, and the companies get sued *less* for poisoning people. This is the strange logic of modern eating.

The science journal *Physics Today* reported in February 2012, "Irradiation does reduce vitamin levels in foods, especially for the B group vitamins. Thiamine is particularly sensitive, and as much as half of that vitamin can be destroyed in food irradiated at high doses. Vitamin loss, however, occurs in many food processes, including cooking and canning."[1] What this says to me is that by the time the producer gets done exposing your food to radiation, and then you cook it, what is left of the nutrition?

GARDENERS TEND TO KNOW EXACTLY WHERE THEIR VEGETABLES HAVE BEEN AND HOW THEY HAVE BEEN TREATED.

The government, by the way, says not to worry too much about nutrient loss via irradiation because they keep a strict control on it—if radiation destroys more than 10 percent of nutrients, they won't allow it to be used. Personally, 10 percent sounds like too much to me. The same article, by the way, claims that irradiated food is nontoxic at low levels, but in 2008 more than a dozen cats in Australia were paralyzed and then died because of eating irradiated cat food.

When you are producing food in your backyard, food contamination is far, far less likely to ever be an issue because the food is not being mass-produced. Gardeners tend to know exactly where their vegetables have been and how they have been treated.

3 Self-Provident Living

Smart families don't rely on the government—fellow taxpayers—to "save" them in a pinch. I grew up milking a cow. My mother made butter in our kitchen with an antique, hand-cranked butter churn given to her by an elderly neighbor. And I'm not that old; this was in the 1980s. She ground wheat to make pancakes for us every morning before school. If we ran out of milk, the nearest grocery story was an hour's drive round-trip—but we had milk coming out our ears! (My father once bartered our fresh, raw milk for new beds for me and my sister.) We had cream, butter, eggs, and meat. (To this day I can't eat steak. I ate so much steak growing up that I can't stand the sight of it anymore. When people comment about that, I tell them I've eaten more steak than they will eat

produce raised on their own property. They teach their children and grandchildren to use credit cards, to eat out, to take out huge loans for cars and houses. They teach them that when they are hungry, they must pay someone for food.

The world is changing. It is time once again to bless our own lives with more self-providence and less dependence on others for food—and it is time to keep more of our hard-earned money in the process. It is time to teach these skills to our children and grandchildren. As I said in the preface to this book, I have raised at least some of my own food no matter where I have lived—condo, college apartment, rental home, and now at our home on an acre and a half. Wherever you live, you can raise at least some of your own food.

Give Yourself a Raise

When the food on your table comes from your garden, you can save big bucks avoiding the grocery store. I was giving a speech about this recently when an accountant in the back of the room interrupted me to say I'd forgotten one important aspect of giving yourself a raise—sales tax. He was right; where I live, that is an immediate 6 percent savings. And with this book, you won't need to waste cash on pricey produce covered in industrial fertilizer and nonsense chemicals that didn't exist when our ancestors were

in their entire lives. I'm retired from steak. Interestingly, my mother feels the same way about eggs—she grew up working in her parents' commercial eggery and had her fill of eggs!)

I didn't know we were self-provident. I thought this was the way everyone lived.

Today, most people are teaching their children and grandchildren something exactly opposite. If the stock market shudders, so do they. Most people have never, ever made an entire meal from completely fresh feeding their families from the backyard garden. This saved money quickly begins to add up. I'm sure most families with children in the United States spend between several hundred and a thousand dollars a month on groceries and eating out. If you cut that money in half, you could use the savings to get out of debt, to help children and neighbors, to give to charity, or to put money toward retirement. Eating from your own garden twelve months a year is no different than getting a raise at work. In fact, it is even better—it is a raise you can give yourself. No begging your tight-fisted boss!

5 Security Against Lost Wages

"Lost wages" is a nice way of talking about being laid off. Not long ago, another friend of mine posted this dreaded and heartbreaking message on Facebook: "Hubby got laid off today . . . if you know of an opening (anywhere) for an incredible civil engineer . . ." I myself was once laid off from a corporate job, many years ago, so I know firsthand how it feels and the panic and fear that comes with it. But there is a measure of peace in self-reliance when it comes to food for the table. At our house, we have been able to make trips to the grocery store the exception, not the rule. There is huge financial peace in that.

Protection from Harsh Weather

One of the crazy things about the world today is that a drought in the Midwest, for example, affects the price of beef across the nation (because beef cattle are fattened on corn). In 2008, flooding in Midwestern states like Iowa and Wisconsin destroyed acres of corn, which newspapers reported drove up the price of gas (because of ethanol), soda pop (corn syrup), and corn chips and beef in the West, where I live.[2] When tomatoes in California freeze in the field— brace yourself—fast food restaurants across the United States are impacted. (Okay, families are impacted too, having to pay higher prices for tomatoes in the grocery store. But that is never what is reported on the nightly news. The nightly news says, "The horror, the horror: McDonald's is suffering from a tomato shortage for hamburgers!") But when you know how to keep a thriving winter garden, as you will learn in this book, then harsh weather around the nation doesn't affect your family's food supply.

7 Economic Depression and Recession

I'll never forget the day, as a kid, that I asked my grandparents, as part of a school assignment, to tell me about growing up during the Great Depression. My beloved grandma looked at me and said, "We didn't

know there was a depression on." At the time, I was disappointed. My assignment was to interview my grandparents and then report back to my teacher the horrors they had experienced. I was sure I was going to get a failing grade on that assignment. But there were no horrors to report. Why? Because, as my grandparents explained, they both grew up exactly like I did: in a rural community on a farm. They were not invested in the stock market, so the great stock market crash had no effect on their lives. There was no sprawling grocery store in the town where they lived—they grew their own food. Their parents had no credit cards because they hadn't been invented. They didn't have

massive mortgages or huge car loans. When my grandpa, Phill Nielson, decided to ask my grandma, Wilhelmina "Billie" Huntsman, to marry him, he first went and bought a house, before he even proposed. You read that right. He had saved up four thousand dollars, and he bought a house. They lived in that house the rest of their lives, and my grandpa was proud that there had never been a mortgage on that house for a single minute, ever.

In my lifetime, I don't ever remember my grandparents buying beef—they had a freezer full of beef from their own cattle. And they gave meat to all their children (my parents raised beef cattle too). My grandparents

Caleb Warnock

never bought eggs; they had chickens. We never had to have chickens because they had so many, they just gave us eggs. We never bought eggs.

If Grandma wanted a tomato, she went to her large garden and got one. If she wanted green beans, she went to the cellar and got a jar full of beans she had grown and canned. She made her own ketchup and her own pickles, and she put up her own corn and beets. All of this is the way she and my grandpa had grown up. They didn't want to rely on others—that would not have been comfortable to them. They lived their entire lives in a town (Lynndyl, Utah) with a grand total of ninety-eight residents and no grocery store. (There was a tiny mom-and-pop's where the locals bought things on a tab. I got in big trouble once for buying ice cream on my parent's tab for a couple weeks while on my way to feed the cows after school each day.) People took care of themselves. And my grandparents taught their children and their grandchildren, including me, to do the same.

8 Commercial Contamination and Shortages

Our modern food system is broken. Many people get sick or die every year from eating food sold in grocery stores. Sadly, a reversal of this trend is unlikely anytime soon.

The problem is that safely producing food on a massive scale has proven impossible to

Death by Cantaloupe

You may remember in late July 2011 when people mysteriously began to die from listeria—a deadly bacteria that normally has nothing to do with cantaloupe. When the outbreak finally ended, 146 people had been sickened in twenty-eight states, and the CDC reported that a staggering 33 people had died, and a woman pregnant at the time of her illness had a miscarriage—all because of eating cantaloupe (Centers for Disease Control and Prevention, "Multistate Outbreak of Listeriosis").

This incident now stands as the deadliest outbreak of foodborne illness in the United States in more than a decade. The deadly melons came from Jensen Farms in southern Colorado, a huge industrial cantaloupe farm. What really caused panic was the fact that the cantaloupes were shipped all over, and the symptoms of listeria can take up to two months to appear. The outside of the melons were contaminated. Just touching them in the store was potentially fatal. If that is not evidence of a broken food system, I don't know what is.

do, especially when the people processing the food are being paid minimum wage and are not invested in food safety. Meanwhile, agro-mega-conglomerates continue to lull us with television commercials showing cute families proudly and attentively growing food for your local grocery store. In reality, the small family farm has ceased to exist. To prove the point, go to your nearest grocery store and ask where the food came from. What country? What state? What farm? Who grew it? When was it picked? What was sprayed on it? How was it handled? Who touched it? No one in the store will be able to answer these questions for you.

Examples like the infobox above are far from rare. Here are some documented examples of grocery store food poisoning:

In October 2011, 68 people across ten states were poisoned by salmonella at Taco Bell restaurants. The CDC took some heat for refusing to reveal the name of the restaurant chain for weeks.

In September 2006, bagged baby spinach was linked to an E. coli outbreak causing the deaths of 3 people and sickening of nearly 200 others.

❄ In September 2011, listeria-contaminated romaine lettuce was shipped to twenty-one states. The contamination was discovered early, the lettuce was recalled, and no one died.

❄ In May 2010, 19 people were poisoned by E. coli from romaine lettuce shipped to twenty-three states.

❄ In June 2008, 161 people in several states were sickened by salmonella on tomatoes. At least 25 people were hospitalized.

I could list pages of similar examples. Such mass poisoning cases have become so common that they only make it into the news if lots of people are made sick or killed! There are cases of industrial food poisoning and mass food recalls in the United States every single day—if you don't believe me, just go to Google News and type "foodborne illness" into the search. But you'll probably want to do it after dinner. Just saying! When you are done reading about the day's grocery store food recalls, type in "garden vegetable poison" or something like it and try to find stories of families being sickened by eating out of their backyard garden. I haven't found any yet.

9 No Artificial Heat or Electricity

The reason you probably bought this book is because you don't believe melons (or fresh tomatoes, lettuce, cucumbers, peas, beans, beets, and so on) can be grown in winter in the West without artificial heat or electricity. I was teaching a winter gardening class recently to about fifty people and a man in the back row interrupted me mid-sentence.

"I've just never heard of this," he said, literally gasping. "Fresh lettuce in January? Are you sure?"

"Well . . . I . . . well"—he was literally stammering now—"I'm not saying I don't believe you, but I just can't believe it. Why have I never heard of this before? Winter lettuce?"

To be honest, I'm dreading this already because I know I'm going to get exactly the same responses when I do signings for this book. There is a chapter about winter gardening in my first book. I was doing a book signing one day, and I mentioned winter gardening. A woman argued with me for ten minutes, saying she was a scientist and that

IT IS TIME TO LEARN AGAIN THE SIMPLE FORGOTTEN SKILLS THAT KEPT THE GENERATIONS BEFORE US ALIVE . . .

I pointed out to him that not only was I sure, but I had brought with me (this was in January) lettuce and tomatoes, beets, chard, carrots, rutabaga and more, all picked in the middle of a snowstorm immediately before I left to teach the class, and paper plates of my vegetables were being passed around the room for the audience to taste as he spoke. "If this is not proof enough," I said, "then come and tour my winter garden yourself. Hundreds of people have." Then, teasing just a little bit, I asked him if he thought that I'd bought all these fresh vegetables from the local grocery store and that I was really trying to play a massive trick on everyone.

winter gardening is scientifically impossible. She actually became upset. When I told her she was welcome to come and tour my winter garden, she stormed off mad. (That's always fun to deal with at a book signing.)

I understand all this incredulity. If the woman had not stomped off, I would have pointed out to her that her great-great-grandmother would have been equally incredulous to know that her kin didn't know how to grow winter lettuce. The real problem is that we have strayed so far from the ability to raise our own food, we now find winter gardening to be unbelievable. But it is true, and it has been done for more than two thousand years. Sometimes when I'm doing book signings in Costco, I say, "After years of intensive research, it turns out there was no Costco here when the pioneers arrived. And they lived!" (Sorry, Costco. Please keep carrying my books!)

Winter gardening is not my invention, not by a long shot. But perhaps it will be my reinvention. Given the economic state of the world, it is high time we reinvent the concept of feeding our families out of our own backyard gardens. It is time to learn again the simple forgotten skills that kept the generations before us alive, before the invention of the grocery store, before Costco, before that dubious modern practice of living paycheck to paycheck, growing only our credit card bills. (I'm proud to say I don't own a credit card.)

6 REASONS TO READ THIS BOOK YOU MIGHT NOT HAVE CONSIDERED

1 Food Prices Are Rising (and You Are Tricked at the Grocery Store)

According to the World Bank's "Food Price Watch," food prices around the globe rose 24 percent in 2011 compared to 2010. That is a huge, frightening increase, and they warned that prices are expected to remain "high and volatile."[3] But most families didn't need that warning—they already knew that.

Perhaps you didn't really notice the price of food jumping. I'll bet, however, that you have noticed yourself going to the grocery

a half ounce at a time. So does cereal. So do tubes of toothpaste. Put your hand on the bottom of anything sold in a rigid plastic container—juice, or cleaning products, to name two—and you'll find a hidden indentation on the bottom of the package, which decreases the space for the actual product inside.

This past fall, my extended family was having Thanksgiving dinner and they asked me to make my grandfather's homemade root beer recipe, which makes five gallons and requires five pounds of sugar. But

A NATION OF FAMILIES THAT DON'T KNOW HOW TO FEED THEMSELVES IN GOOD TIMES IS GOING TO BE DESPERATE IN A TIME OF NEED.

store more than ever. That's because you, and your wallet, are being tricked.

Here is a dirty little secret of the food industry—as prices go up, the price in the store often stays the same.

Huh? How is this possible?

Here's how: The packages of food get smaller and lighter. And not always in ways that are obvious. Bags of chips get smaller

when I went to the grocery store to buy five pounds of sugar—which I have used to make this recipe for years—all the bags had been changed to four pounds. But the price hadn't changed. Ice cream, laundry detergent, juices, flour, pancake mixes, jams and jellies, peanut butter, salad—slowly, the packages are all getting smaller. So you end up going to the store *a lot* more often. And having to go to the store more often hurts families in another way—the more you go to the store, the more impulse purchases you make. And it costs more in gas to return to the grocery store more often.

When you grow your own dinner, you go to the store less often. You spend less. You get more exercise working in the garden. You are happier. I know I'm happier in the garden and at the dinner table, eating free, delicious, organic, minutes-old food.

2 National Security Is Rooted in the Garden

Remember victory gardens? In World War II, food was so scarce that it was rationed, just like gasoline, tires, and clothes. Factories were devoted to the war effort, not freezing and canning food (both had only recently become popular). The government started a huge campaign to encourage families to grow backyard "victory gardens." We had to feed ourselves and our troops. We could not rely on imports, and we could not rely on the grocery store—store shelves would have been bare without ration cards. (I take an original World War II "War Ration Book One" with me to my speeches to show audiences.)

Let us pray that this nation never again sees such dark, terrible days. But a nation of families that don't know how to feed themselves in good times is going to be desperate in a time of need, and that will not strengthen our national security, to say the least.

Worse yet, during World War II our nation was not nearly as removed from year-round backyard gardening and garden know-how as we are today. If the worst happened today, could we feed ourselves? (If you would like to see one of the government's original World War II film reels teaching people to plant victory gardens, visit my blog, caleb-warnock.blogspot.com, and search for the "Dig for Victory" post.)

If You Give Kids Seeds, Kids Will Love Vegetables

If I ran the world, every child would get vegetable seeds in their stockings for Christmas. (Open-pollinated seeds, of course. I don't use any hybrids, for reasons explained in my first book.) When I was young, I was so jealous of my cousins because my aunt and uncle would give each of them a small garden plot every spring, and the kids would get to plant whatever they wanted in their plot. It was their job to care for that little patch of garden and later in the summer use it to make a family meal. When I would go to visit my cousins, we would run out into their backyard, and they would each show me their garden patch. I wanted a garden patch of my own! But my parents never grew much of a garden because my grandparents had a huge garden and lived nearby, so it wasn't necessary.

At our house, I let the little kids have their own garden patch like my cousins did, and they love it. Better yet, they eat the food they grow. When a child grows carrots and beans and corn and radishes, they eat carrots and beans and corn and radishes. They are proud of their garden, and they love "their" vegetables.

Over the past few years, there have been a spate of cookbooks teaching parents how to hide vegetables in everyday meals so the kids don't know what they are eating. If parents would just take their kids out into the garden, that problem would go away forever. And kids eating out of the garden is far, far better than kids drinking soda while watching television and playing video games. Don't get me started.

One last note about kids in the garden. Xander, who has just turned six years old as I write this, owns no fewer than four shovels. I bought him his first shovel when he was two years old. Now his little sister uses it. I took Xander to my favorite local nursery, which stocks real children's garden tools (not plastic shovels but real wood and metal shovels for children), and I let Xander pick out his first shovel. It wasn't his birthday, it wasn't Christmas; it was simply a nice day for gardening. The best ten bucks I ever spent.

Today, he knows how to plant seeds, how to harvest vegetables, how to water, how to dig. He is healthy and eats good food that he grows himself. He has a sense of pride in his little garden and in mine. And he loves

Caleb Warnock

to work side by side with me in the garden, whether it's winter or summer. Last week, his teacher asked us to bring some of our chickens to his class, and in the spring, his entire class is coming to our little farm (yes, we are what passes for a family farm today) for a three-hour field trip. Kids who grow up in a garden are far more likely to turn into adults who eat in a garden—and those adults are far more likely to be healthy, in my experience. So give the kids and grandkids seeds in their Christmas stockings, and then teach the kids how to put those seeds to work. And with the way the world is turning, they might be grateful, one day, that they know how to feed themselves in hard times.

Thousands of Years of Work Are Being Lost

Quietly, and almost unnoticed, the vast majority of our heirloom food varieties have now been lost. In the lettuce chapter of this book, I write about one particularly hard loss: the world's very best winter lettuce that I have literally searched the world for, to no avail.

The vegetables, fruits, and meats we eat today are the result of the careful and fastidious selection of traits over centuries. In my first book, I explain how carrots were originally white, purple, and yellow, and only most recently were bred to be orange. I grow some of the rarest vegetables in the world in my garden—mangels, winter

onions, winter spinach, and winter lettuces, for instance. Winter vegetables are the most rare of all vegetables.

96% of the commercial vegetables available in 1903 are now extinct (Center for Biodiversity and Conservation, "Biodiversity and Your Food"). And eight of the fifteen breeds of pigs raised in the United States fifty years ago are now extinct, along with a staggering sixty breeds of chickens that were raised in the United States prior to World War II (American Livestock Breeds Conservancy, "Rare Breed Facts").

Years ago, as grocery stores became more available, fewer families needed to spend the time required to raise their own vegetables and protein. Even fewer worked to continue pure breeding lines, both in animals and vegetables. As backyard gardens began to die out, so did entire varieties of garden seeds. That is because seeds only exist if they are grown in the garden. Seed companies only grow seeds that sell, and agri-conglomerates only buy a narrow selection of seeds for vegetables that will travel long distances, don't bruise, and can sit on store shelves. So we've

lost almost all the heirloom, open-pollinated vegetables (the kind you can't patent).

Today, much of the seed used around the world is hybrid, meaning that if you take a seed from your garden, that seed will likely be sterile or produce fruit that does not resemble the parent. Such seed requires home gardeners to purchase new seed each season and removes the ability to provide their own seed from year to year. If you are interested, my first book has a lot more information about this.

A group of people around the world is now working to save the rare vegetable seeds that are left. In 1975, Diane Ott Whealy's terminally ill grandfather gave her and her husband, Kent Whealy, the seeds of two heirloom garden plants: a flower variety and a pink-fleshed tomato from Germany, brought over by his parents from Bavaria when they immigrated to St. Lucas, Iowa, in the 1870s. Struck by the gift they had been given and recognizing that if they did not continue the line, both varieties would quickly be lost, the Whealys founded Seed Savers Exchange in 1975.[4] They didn't know it then, but the couple had single-handedly started a small volunteer movement to save what remained of the world's homegrown, open-pollinated seed. Much of this seed is available nowhere else.

Today, eleven thousand members around the world, including me, participate in the nonprofit Exchange and have mailed over one million seed samples to one another. Many of the seeds offered were once sold commercially but have been discontinued, and they would have been lost without private gardeners keeping the seed lines alive. For information, visit seedsavers.org.

5 Overwintering Is Required for Seed Saving

Few people grow their own garden seed today, instead of buying seed. This means that few people know that some seeds—especially root vegetables—require two years to produce true seed. Learning how to keep vegetables over winter is one part of learning to grow your own garden seed, which saves you more money and makes you more self-sufficient.

6 Only Living Knowledge Will Benefit the Next Generations

Though it pains me to write this sentence, a book is not good enough. My goal in writing this book is to help families feed themselves twelve months a year. But waiting until there is a crisis in the world or in your family finances is too late. We need to keep a working knowledge alive. Winter gardening, just like summer gardening, is not foolproof. There can be a learning curve. And as hard as I try to put every detail in this book that you will need to know to grow a winter garden, nothing beats a little personal experience. I have a living memory of my great-grandmother, who always fed herself and her family out of her garden for her whole life. You might remember someone in your own family who had that skill too. But the generations after us will have absolutely no living memory of such things—unless they see *us* in *our* gardens. Winter gardening is all but extinct in the United States. We are the only ones who can keep a working knowledge of this skill alive and give that living knowledge to the following generations.

Notes

1. Dickson, "Radiation Meets Food," 66.

2. Isidore, "How the Floods Will Hurt the Economy."

3. "Food Price Watch—January 2012," The World Bank.

4. "About Us," Seed Savers Exchange.

CALEB'S TOP TEN "CANNOT LIVE WITHOUT"
WINTER GARDEN VEGETABLES

If I were a pilgrim journeying to a new world and I could only choose ten seed varieties to take with me, these would be them. For information on why these are great for winter and how to grow them, see the relevant sections of this book. All of these are open-pollinated seed varieties. As I said before, I do not grow hybrid seed in my garden. My top ten winter garden vegetables:

1. **Winter Green Jewel romaine** (a super-hardy winter variant of Parris Island Cos lettuce developed by me)

2. **Purple-top globe turnip**

3. **Extra dwarf pak choi**

4. **Swiss chard** (any variety)

5. **Cascadia pea**

6. **Joan rutabaga**

7. **Siberian kale**

8. **Yellow Spanish onion**

9. **Carrots** (any variety)

10. **Turkey Red winter wheat**

Runner-up: Mangels. These are not for human consumption, but they have been used for hundreds of years as winter feed for livestock. I feed them to my horse and cows in winter as a supplement.

(AND FOR FUN) CALEB'S TOP TEN "CANNOT LIVE WITHOUT"
SUMMER GARDEN VEGETABLES

For information on why these are great, and how to grow them, see my first book, *The Forgotten Skills of Self-Sufficiency Used by the Mormon Pioneers.*

1. **Noir des Carmes cantaloupe**

2. **Albino** (white sugar) **beet**

3. **Rampicante Italian vining zucchini**

4. **Raspberries**

5. **Chioggia beet**

6. **Longkeeper tomatoes**

7. **Boule d'Or turnip**

8. **Sweet basil**

9. **Stevia**

10. **Purple podded pole bean**

Runners up: Connecticut field pumpkin, Egyptian walking onion, oregano, lemon balm, Yukon Gold potato, Snow Fairy tomato, Concord grape vines, Elberta or Red Haven peach, a storage variety of watermelon, a great cucumber.... (Any avid gardener would be hard pressed to choose just ten!)

EASY WINTER GARDENING
WHERE TO GET STARTED

Most people have never planted a winter garden before—or ever even seen one. So if you are brand-new to this, where do you get started?

The goal of winter gardening is to eat fresh vegetables in the bitter cold months of the year. This means *harvesting* in winter, not planting. This chapter will tell you how to start: the easiest vegetables to plant in spring, summer, and fall for fresh backyard eating all winter long. Then I will tell you some of the easiest things to plant in winter for super-early spring eating.

IF IT IS SPRING:

You can and should plant vegetables in your spring garden for fresh winter eating later; some vegetables need the entire growing season to be mature for winter eating. Here are three of the easiest examples (for full instructions, see the related chapters of this book):

- carrots (any heirloom variety)
- Swiss chard (any heirloom variety)
- extra dwarf pak choi (a miniature variety of Chinese cabbage. If you plant it once in spring and let some go to seed, you get to eat it twice—in spring and winter.)

IF IT IS SUMMER:

It's hard to think about winter gardening in the heat of summer, among all the summer harvest. But some winter vegetables must be planted in summer if you want to harvest them fresh in winter. Here are three of the easiest:

- early cabbage varieties
- America spinach
- beets (any heirloom variety)

IF IT IS FALL:

Autumn is the most important time in winter gardening. Just like planting in spring to eat in summer, most of the vegetables you eat from the winter garden must be planted in autumn. Here are three of the easiest:

- Cascadia peas or Tom Thumb peas
- Osaka Purple mustard greens
- green romaine or oak leaf lettuce

IF IT IS WINTER:

Nothing cures cabin fever in the coldest, snowiest months of the year quite like sprouting new vegetable plants! Here are three of the easiest:

- Swiss chard (any heirloom variety)
- Noir des Carmes cantaloupe (in February)
- Blue Solaise or Belgian Breeder's Winter Mix leeks

HOW THE WINTER SOLSTICE AFFECTS SPROUTING WINTER VEGETABLES

There are some winter vegetables you just won't have any luck sprouting before January. This is because those vegetables respond to the winter solstice. (Don't be confused. Mature garden plants will be just fine. I'm talking about sprouting seeds.)

The winter solstice is the longest night of the year—and therefore the shortest day of the year—and it occurs in the days just before Christmas (the exact day is different every year; it ranges from December 22 to December 24). After the winter solstice, the hours of daylight begin to grow day by day, and this is a signal to plants. Another signal to plants is the temperature of the soil, which is directly affected by the amount and strength of daylight. Once the winter solstice has passed, the sunlight begins to get stronger and last longer each day, and this in turn begins to warm the earth, albeit slowly.

In the winter garden, the winter solstice means two things. First, some seeds just won't sprout until after the solstice, or if they do sprout, they will die. This is because until the solstice, the number of daylight hours is reducing day by day, which is a clear signal to seeds and plants (believe it or not) that they are not in the right season for sprouting and beginning life. To them, it's like waking up in the middle of the night and realizing there are hours to go before the day begins—so you go back to bed.

Second, even if you can put your plants in a geothermal greenhouse where you know they will not freeze, the soil is still going to chill (but not freeze) at night even though it may be quite warm during the day. This is equally true in cold frames and hotbeds. This nighttime chill is caused by the number of hours of night—and after the winter solstice, the night is still longer than the day, even though the number of daylight hours is now growing. So even if you can get your sprouts warm during the day, they grow only very slowly because at night the soil is not as warm as it would be if it were really summer. The plants think that something

all summer will continue to grow all winter if you put a cold frame over it in October or November. Just don't expect to sprout Swiss chard (or much else) from seed in November and see it thrive. And even the mature chard in the cold frame will double its growth rate once February arrives, in response to the increasing daylight and warmth.

After the solstice, everything in the winter garden will begin to grow faster (unfortunately, this is also true of winter-hardy weeds, like perennial broadleaf grasses). Slowly, as the strength and amount of daylight increases, the lowest nighttime temperature of the soil in the cold frame, hotbed,

AFTER THE SOLSTICE, EVERYTHING IN THE WINTER GARDEN WILL BEGIN TO GROW FASTER.

funny is going on, and they are right. A hotbed, greenhouse, or cold frame can use the sun to collect warmth, but at night, the temperature plummets again.

These two phenomena are the reason that plants grow and sprout slowly in winter. Some vegetables will sprout regardless of the solstice, like lettuce and peas; however, they will grow slowly until the winter solstice has passed. But again, don't be confused. *Mature* garden plants will be just fine. For example, Swiss chard that has been growing

and greenhouse will rise. In mid- to late February, that nighttime soil temperature seems to hit a critical mass, and suddenly plants in the hotbed, cold frame, and greenhouse begin to grow much faster. And seeds that you had planted weeks earlier and given up hope on suddenly sprout in the hotbed. My favorite example of this is my Grand Rapids lettuce, which grows slowly and steadily in my hotbeds all winter, but in February, it suddenly grows an inch a week. Yes—an inch a week.

WHERE TO BUY SEED
FOR WINTER VEGETABLE VARIETIES

CALEB WARNOCK SEEDS

I never dreamed I would be selling garden seed, but I found myself selling my own seeds by popular demand—as I began teaching winter garden classes, and letting hundreds of people tour my winter and summer gardens, people have wanted my seeds because they have been able to see the garden in action, and they trust that it has been tested for winter growing. And because many winter varieties have become so uncommon, I have some of the rarest seed in the world, and I work to develop brand-new winter varieties, such as my Winter Green Jewel romaine. These varieties were developed in my winter garden and are sold by no one else but me. I also sell pure, open-pollinated, organic seed for a variety of winter and summer vegetables that have been trialed in my garden. For more information, visit caleb-warnock.blogspot.com.

SEED SAVERS EXCHANGE

SSE is the single most important source of heirloom seed in the world, and that is no exaggeration. This is not a commercial corporation. It is a nonprofit group of more than ten thousand volunteers from around the world, including me, who grow their own backyard garden seed and offer it to the other members of SSE. SSE also has a large farm in Decorah, Iowa, where a team of people work to make sure that the rarest open-pollinated seeds in the world are kept viable in living gardens, so that fresh seed is regularly grown out in batches large enough to maintain genetic vigor with a precise eye to purity. The value of this work cannot be overstated. I urge anyone reading this book to become a member of Seed Savers Exchange—this will give you access to the annual seed yearbook. This book has tens of thousands of varieties of open-pollinated vegetable seeds that are available absolutely nowhere else in the world. In many cases, there is only one person left in the world growing out the seed! There is a huge, huge need for more serious, talented gardeners to jump into this group and join the work of keeping alive the heirloom seed heritage. But even if you are not a member, you can order a limited variety of seeds available to the public. For more information, visit seedsavers.org.

BAKER CREEK HEIRLOOM SEEDS

I love this company for many reasons. First of all, they have always sold only open-pollinated, heirloom seed—long before it was trendy. And they test their seed to make sure it has not been corrupted by pollen from genetically modified plants (which is why this company sells very little sweet corn seed—they have only been able to find three or four pure varieties—an enormously sad commentary on what is happening to our food supply and how fast it is happening). And the owners of this company are passionate about seed heritage (you can read their story on their website). Visit rareseeds.com.

WILD GARDEN SEED

This is one of the few commercial seed companies working to improve standard open-pollinated seed and create new varieties. They created my favorite rutabaga, "Joan," and you know that if a company is working to create a new rutabaga (quite possibly the most neglected vegetable in the United States) then Wild Garden Seed cares about gardeners and seed! In the modern world, creating new open-pollinated varieties is like creating great art and then giving the world the copyright for free. I'm grateful for Wild Garden Seed. Visit wildgardenseed.com.

FERTILE VALLEY SEED

This is a tiny seed company owned by renowned plant breeder Carol Deppe, who literally wrote the book teaching everyday gardeners how to develop new varieties of open-pollinated seed. I would never have been able to create my own varieties without her book. She only sells seeds a few months a year—and only a handful of varieties. For information, visit caroldeppe.com.

Get started on your self-sufficient winter garden with

FREE WINTER LETTUCE SEED
from the author, Caleb Warnock!

Simply send an e-mail to calebwarnock@yahoo.com
to request your free seed!

•CLOCHES•

"Cloches.—This name for 'bell glasses' has become almost an English word now, so it may be retained without inconvenience in this work. Cloches have been in constant use in French gardens since about the year 1623—nearly three hundred years—although originally they are said to have come from Italy. . . . The cloches are made of clear glass with a slightly bluish tint as a protection against strong sunshine. Formerly cloches had a knob on top, but as this acted like a lens and burned the plants beneath, those without knobs are now preferred, and generally used. It has been computed that something like five or six millions are in use in French gardens. . . .

"By the use of cloches the gardener is enabled not only to protect tender plants from the cold and wet during the worst period of the year, but owing to the genial temperature beneath them, he can also raise his plants more quickly than in the open air in the ordinary way. By constant use over the plants, having due regard to ventilation and shading, each cloche serves all the purposes of a miniature forcing house."

(Weathers, *French Market-Gardening*, 1909, 34–35, 37–38)

COLD FRAMES
FOR WINTER HARVESTS

For more than two thousand years, winter gardeners have relied on cold frames. A cold frame is a miniature greenhouse—some kind of simple covering for vegetables grown directly in the backyard garden soil in areas where freezing temperatures normally kill the vegetable garden in winter.

When it comes to cold frames, many options exist, ranging from free to expensive:

CLOCHES (also called bell jars)

These are thick glass domes with a single glass knob handle at the top. Cloches were historically used to cover small circles of lettuce or radishes, for example, or larger vegetables, such as a single cauliflower plant. These glass domes had no holes in them and were propped with small pieces of wood on warm winter days to keep the plants inside from dying of heat. Two to three hundred years ago, millions of cloches were used to grow winter vegetables around Paris each winter to feed the city—and London and New York City and every other major city before the invention of industrial food and grocery stores. Today, those antique cloches are highly prized by collectors and have become extremely expensive and hard to find. New cloches are now being manufactured, but they are also expensive and mostly considered to be decorative and not for actual gardening (because they cost so much, not because they don't work. However, the glass in modern cloches is not as thick as the historic cloches, I have noticed).

There are many cheaper modern alternatives. Some gardeners cut the top off of huge, plastic watercooler jugs, turn them upside down, and use them in winter or early spring gardens as free cloches. Some people use plastic sheeting to make a kind of three-sided teepee around plants, especially to extend the life of tomato plants in autumn. Some people say these should have a small hole in the top; others disagree.

I was recently at an auction of antiques where someone was selling a large, white cut glass cover for a fancy ceiling light. I bought it for thirty-five dollars and have used it all winter as a cloche in my garden for mustard greens, peas, and winter spinach. Perhaps because the glass is white, and not clear, the vegetables have grown more slowly than the same vegetables in my cold frames.

With all that said, this is my opinion of cloches, whether old glass, new glass, free plastic, or anything in between: they are too small. They are best left for winter garden experiments, in my opinion. And they don't let enough air in—the plants inside tend to struggle a bit. They just don't work as well as larger cold frames and hotbeds.

GLASS HOUSES (also called terrariums, conservatories, and orangeries)

Glass houses are what they sound like—small "houses" made of glass. I bought mine at a local antiques auction. (Okay, I admit, I enjoy auctions. I buy a lot of garden things at auction. For example, an authentic pioneer hoe made of iron with a ten-foot handle. And a wrought iron circular pole bean trellis. Auctions are what gardeners do for fun!)

The first modern-style greenhouse is believed to have been built at the Vatican using glass in the thirteenth century. This

Greenhouses in the Time of Christ

Tiberius was the second emperor of the Roman Empire. He was born forty-two years before Christ and lived to be seventy-seven years old. In garden circles he is famous today for being the first known person in the world to use a greenhouse. His servants used sheets of mica—a flat, glass-like mineral—to create a greenhouse for growing cucumbers. In *The Natural History of Pliny* (Book XIX, Chapter 23), Pliny the Elder claims Tiberius loves cucumbers: "Indeed, he was never without [them]; for he had raised beds made in frames upon wheels, by means of which the cucumbers were moved and exposed to the full heat of the sun; while, in winter, they were withdrawn, and placed under the protection of frames glazed with mirrorstone."

(Pliny the Elder, *The Natural History of Pliny*, 156)

building, which no longer stands, was built to house exotic plants brought as gifts to the Catholic Church. The technology spread across Italy and then Europe. Some ancient greenhouses were heated though winter nights with wood fires—a practice that has continued in some cases to modern times.

Glass houses became all the rage in the nineteenth century, reaching their height of fame when the Crystal Palace was created in London. The wealthy first started building grand glass houses for winter gardening and keeping exotic tropical plants. Universities were not far behind, using the houses for research and keeping tropical plant specimens. The French called their glass houses "orangeries" because they became popular for growing orange trees and pineapples in winter. (I have both an orange tree and a pineapple plant in my geothermal greenhouse. The lure is irresistible!)

In the vegetable garden, small glass houses were used for winter vegetable growing and early spring vegetable forcing. Today they cost several hundred dollars (unless you buy one at auction like I did for forty bucks) and they are used mostly for indoor, decorative houseplant growing.

Because it is so tall, my glass house loses heat much more easily than my cold frames that hug the ground. Nevertheless, it grows a nice crop of lettuce all winter. And it looks great! In my garden, my glass house is a favorite of visitors. My wife thinks I should

bring it in the house. I think the little kids would break the glass in about ten minutes. For practical gardeners, a glass house is best used as a winter covering for vegetables planted in autumn. Just set the glass house over the vegetables you want to protect from frost, wind, and snow.

Cold Frames for Winter Harvests

SIMPLE COLD FRAMES

Simple cold frames are wooden boxes topped with glass or rigid plastic (the glass lids are historically called "sashes" or "lights"). You can buy a cold frame in any garden catalog or online store, but the problem with them is that they are expensive—150 dollars—and far too tall. They often come with sides a foot tall or more. This means your frame has a lot of surface area exposed to the wind and lots of space to lose the very heat you are trying to conserve.

Today, after experimenting and consulting with other gardeners, I think I have invented the world's cheapest and most efficient winter garden frames, which work equally well for both cold frames and hotbeds for young and small plants.

Here is the big reveal (drum roll . . .) you screw together four pieces of two-by-four studs into a rectangle and cover them with polycarbonate plastic.

Why it took so long to come up with this, I don't know. The key to a happy cold frame or hotbed in winter is to keep the heat near the ground, near the plants. Frames made of two-by-four lumber are very shallow. They don't get blown away in the raging windstorms we get where I live. They cost almost nothing, they can be made very quickly, and they are super efficient—far better at trapping the heat than all the other frames, that I have tried, even the expensive ones.

To construct this simple frame, you don't need anything fancy. You can get twin-wall, polycarbonate plastic (rigid greenhouse material—it's kind of like cardboard made of clear plastic) at almost any garden or hardware store; if they don't have it in stock, they will order it for you. Make a rectangle of two-by-fours—about four feet long and two feet deep works well. Screw the rigid plastic to the top with a few screws (any old screws in the bottom of your kitchen junk drawer will do fine). Pound a nail partway in to make a handle. And you are done. When I first started making these, I used the special screws with the rubber gasket, and I sealed the plastic to the wood with caulk and bought nifty little ceramic knob handles—none of this is necessary, I've learned. The frames work equally as well if you use a few old screws and some leftover wood.

And even building a frame is not necessary. I've had equal success going to the local thrift store, buying a used table with a glass top for five dollars, throwing away all but the glass, and laying the glass over a hotbed (instructions for creating a hotbed are in the next chapter). I put a little dirt around the edges to lift the glass off the ground, and I have an instant frame, super-cheap, super-easy. And it works equally as well as all my other frames.

A couple of winter vegetables will require a taller frame: cabbages and Swiss chard. For these, you can add another layer of two-by-fours to your frame to double the height.

One more thing. Anytime you read in this book about a "lid" or "cover" or "frame" for a hotbed or a cold frame, I'm talking about the frame I have just described here, which works perfectly for either a hotbed or a cold frame.

The Crystal Palace

The Crystal Palace was an enormous greenhouse built of cast iron and plate glass in London's Hyde Park for the Great Exhibition of 1851—now considered to be the first world's fair. At the time, mass-produced plate glass was a new invention. The palace was a third of a mile long, and had a ceiling 128 feet tall. Full-sized trees were housed inside, complete with sparrows. At the time, it was the largest glass building ever built, covering nineteen acres. More than four thousand tons of wrought and cast iron were used, along with nine hundred thousand square feet of glass. After the exhibition, it was moved and enlarged and called a "Winter Park and Garden Under Glass." Queen Victoria presided at the re-opening, and the building drew more than two million visitors a year. In its new location it featured a historic swamp complete with model dinosaurs. But after several decades, it fell into disrepair. Facing enormous upkeep costs, owners declared bankruptcy. In 1936 it was destroyed by fire. For more information, visit crystalpalacefoundation.org.uk.

ALL-NATURAL HOTBEDS
FOR WINTER GARDENING

Like cold frames, naturally heated hotbeds have been used for gardening for at least four hundred years, if not much longer. You can make a hotbed in minutes.

This is what you will need:

❄ A spot in your garden that gets good winter sun (without shade).

❄ Either green manure or green leafy material for natural heating.

❄ Some compost or good soil in which to grow your plants.

❄ A lid made of glass or plastic.

The concept is simple—you need to warm a garden bed in winter to grow things that cannot grow in frozen earth. To be successful, a hotbed must have a source of daytime heat, and a source of nighttime heat. A lid made of glass or plastic will provide daytime heat.

Green animal manure or green leafy material in the bottom of your hotbed provides nighttime warmth while it decomposes. Both will work, but here are some considerations to keep in mind:

GREEN ANIMAL MANURE

Manure from any livestock animal (horse, cow, chicken, rabbit, pig, goat) will work, as long as it is relatively fresh—no more than a month old. Manure that has been sitting around a while has already begun to decompose, and the heat in your hotbed must last the entire winter. On the other hand, fresh manure, when buried in the ground, will heat your hotbed all winter. Old manure

•HOTBEDS•

"From October till the end of March hot-beds are in constant use for the production of early crops. As some of these require more heat than others it is necessary to regulate the thickness and heat of the beds according to the season and the crop grown. . . .

"French growers usually make three different kinds of beds according to season and crop—namely, (1) raised hot-beds; (2) sunken beds in trenches for melons; and (3) in April beds made from spent manure or the dark mould that has already played its part in the production of previous crops.

"Having marked out by means of pegs and lines where the beds and frames and cloches are to be placed—bearing in mind that they are to be inclined towards the south, south-east, or south-west—the manure is wheeled on to the ground or carried on the back in the peculiar wicker baskets called "hottes". . . .

". . . Beds made during the winter months are also thicker in proportion than those made in autumn or spring, as greater heat is required to resist the atmospheric cold. . . .

". . . When sufficient manure has been placed in position, it should be trodden down well with the feet . . . to secure a level surface and equal density throughout. Any hollow places must be filled up with more manure, until the proper level has been reached. When complete, the whole bed should be watered all over if inclined to be dry, so that it is made moist enough to generate a steady heat.

"When making beds in October for the cultivation of Lettuces, they need not be more than 8 in. in depth. A fair quantity of short litter should be mixed with the hot and fresh manure, because at this period the plants do not require heat so much as being kept rather dry and sufficiently warm. Beds made in November should be somewhat deeper, and made with equal parts of old and fresh manure. From the commencement of December the beds should be from 12 to 14 in. thick, and made of fresher manure. This is necessary, as a greater and more steady heat is then required for such crops as Lettuces, early Carrots, and Turnips. . . .

". . . When the frames are in position, the 'lights' are placed upon them, and these are covered with mats for a few days to hasten the more rapid heating of the manure in the dark."

(Weathers, *French Market-Gardening*, 1909, 20–23)

could finish the decomposition too early, so in this case, "fairly fresh" is important.

At our house, we have chickens, a horse, cows, and rabbits. I have used manure from all of these animals in hotbeds. When I want to make a hotbed, I simply go out into the pasture or the chicken coop with a bucket and get the freshest manure I can find. It usually takes me about two five-gallon buckets of manure—roughly filled, not compacted—to fill a hotbed that is three feet by two feet.

You want the manure to be relatively compacted so that your twelve inches of manure is fairly dense. You can do this by pushing it down with the back of a shovel. Or if you have pasture boots, you can tromp it down inside the hole. Please note that your hole should be roughly sixteen inches deep, and your manure should be about twelve inches high, so when you are done, your manure should not completely fill your hole.

GREEN LEAFY MATERIAL

This option is for people who might not be able to find access to livestock manure, or people who feel squeamish about using manure for whatever reason. You can use any green leafy material you can get your hands on—weeds, garden plants, leaves from your trees. Don't use the roots; they tend to like the warmth too much, and they begin to grow slowly—especially hardy perennial pasture grasses and weeds. Because this leafy green material is not nearly as dense as animal manure, it will sink down in your hole over time as it decomposes. This means your vegetables will sink too. The material will probably not sink evenly, so slowly what began as a level, flat garden bed in your hotbed will turn into a concave hole. Your sinking garden is not really a problem—just be prepared for this reality. To keep this sinking to a minimum, you will need to use a shovel to vigorously chop up your green leafy material when you first put it in the hole. The more you chop, the more dense you can make the leaves, and the less they will sink over time. Just be aware that even vigorously chopped green leaves are still going to sink at least by half—so if you start with twelve inches, the center will eventually sink six inches or more. Again, this is not a problem, but it looks kind of odd as spring approaches. On the other hand, it's fun to see the clear evidence that decomposition is at work underneath your hotbed!

All-Natural Hotbeds for Winter Gardening

STEP-BY-STEP INSTRUCTIONS FOR MAKING A HOTBED AND A COMPLETE EXPLANATION OF HOW AND WHY THIS WORKS

1 Dig a hole. Soil absorbs the heat of the sun during the day and slowly releases that heat during the night. Your hotbed will collect this heat most efficiently if it resembles a shallow hole when it is done. This is because the more surface area of soil you expose, the more heat you collect. Therefore, you start with a hole.

Before digging, choose a location that will get as much winter sunlight as possible. Dig your hole about sixteen inches deep. The width of the hole should be slightly smaller than the size of your lid.

2 Fill the hole with about twelve inches of green manure, or green leafy material, and compact. Both fresh manure and fresh green leaves of any kind will decompose over the winter, slowly releasing heat. This heat is primarily necessary to keep the garden plants in your hotbed alive during the night.

There is an important exception: melons, squashes, tomatoes, and beans will not survive if you use only a foot of manure—this doesn't release enough heat for them. For these four vegetables, you will need to dig a hole three feet deep and fill it with green manure.

3 On top of your manure or leafy greens in the hole, add three to six inches of compost or loamy garden soil (I usually use about three inches). This will be your growing medium. Plant your seeds and water them generously. This deep watering will help activate the manure below so it begins to decompose and produce heat for the winter.

4 Cover your hotbed frame with a lid constructed of glass or rigid plastic. The lid does not have to be level. You can even mound the dirt slightly on the north end to tilt the lid toward the southern winter sun. Roughly seal the edge with loose dirt. In my experience, the edges do not need to be completely sealed against the weather—the hotbed garden seems to happily tolerate a little air flow, without being affected even on those seventeen-below-zero winter nights.

WATERING YOUR HOTBED

You will need to open the hotbed roughly every two or three weeks to water by hand. Even in December and January, a cold frame or hotbed can get relatively warm during the day. So if your vegetables begin to look like they are suffering, don't assume they are suffering from the cold. They are more likely in need of water.

You don't need to water every week. I find that watering about every three weeks is okay, but you have to keep an eye out. If it becomes unusually warm, water them every two weeks.

Never water in the morning or evening in winter. The ideal time to water is between noon and 3 p.m. because this will be the warmest part of the day. This gives the beds a couple of hours of sunlight before dusk to warm up again and gives the ground time to absorb the water before night falls and the temperatures plummet. Choose a relatively warm day to open the cold frames or hotbeds for watering. Close them as soon as you are done watering. While the beds are open is also a good time to harvest your vegetables.

37

QUESTIONS & ANSWERS

Q: Can I use clear plastic film for the lid of my hotbed or cold frame, instead of glass or rigid plastic?

I wouldn't recommend it. Plastic film tends to collapse and rip in the wind. If the plastic rips during a windy night, all the vegetables inside will die. The risk is not worth it. And remember, if you have children in your garden, glass might not be the best choice either. Or if you happen to have a lot of visitors to your garden, like I do. My frameless glass lids were all stepped on by visitors and broken. Erg!

Q: When can I plant my hotbed or cold frame?

Anytime during the winter. Growth in winter will be slow, so plan your planting calendar accordingly. You will want to plant some things in the fall and some in summer so they can get a head start on growth and be ready to be eaten in winter. See the individual vegetable chapters for details.

Q: Can I plant seeds directly in the hotbed in December and January?

Yes. Keep in mind, these seeds should be winter varieties (see vegetable chapters for

specific variety recommendations). Seeds will germinate much more slowly in winter than in summer when sown directly in the soil of the hotbed. Don't be surprised if germination takes two to three weeks or even longer. And notice the question was for hotbeds, not cold frames. You cannot plant seeds in cold frames in deepest winter.

Q: Can I start seeds in the house and transplant them to a hotbed or cold frame?

Yes. Especially in November, December, January, and February. This will give your hotbed or cold frame a jump start. The key to success is to move the seedlings outside as soon as they sprout in the house. The longer you wait before taking them outside once they have sprouted, the more likely they are to go into shock. Seedlings that have just begun to emerge from the soil or have emerged within the past twenty-four hours will do the best outside. This may seem counter-intuitive—these tiny, new seedlings look extremely fragile. But the longer they stay in the house, the harder it will be for them to acclimatize outside. Also, seedlings from the house will have a much better survival rate if you transplant them to a hotbed instead of a cold frame.

Q: Can I use the manure from my dog or cat to heat my hotbed?

Meh. I get asked this question more than any other when it comes to hotbeds. My answer is no. For a couple of reasons. First, in this day and age rare is the pet that does not have some kind of medication in them. Our pets are not really "organic," so to speak, so you have to think twice about what happens to those contaminates in the garden. Second, unless you have a lot of cats or dogs, you are going to have trouble collecting enough fresh manure in a short enough time frame to fill your hotbed. Finally, while I have no problem gardening with manure from barnyard animals, somehow using dog and cat manure seems . . . wrong. But it's your garden.

Q: When should I build my hotbed?

Probably no earlier than September—if you put in your natural heat too early, it may not last all winter. Beginning in September,

KNOWLEDGE FROM HISTORIC GARDENS AND GARDENERS

"As one might expect, coverings of mats or sacks were in use to protect plants long before even cloches or frames were thought of. In these days the mats mostly in use are made of rye straw. Each mat is about 5 ft. to 6 ft. 6 in. long, and 4 ft. 6 in. wide, weighs about 11 or 12 lb., and is kept together by means of five strings running across the straw stems. Before use the mats are steeped in a solution of copper sulphate not only to preserve them, but also to prevent rats and mice from gnawing them, and to keep off fungoid diseases. . . .

"The mats are useful not only for protecting the plants in the frames or under the cloches from severe frosts in winter, but in summer time they are almost as much in evidence for shading the lights and cloches from the scorching rays of the sun. Old mats are useful for covering the cloches that are stacked up in summer, to protect them against the sudden hailstorms that often do much damage. Although the rye-straw mats are reasonably cheap, it may be worth while to make them in gardens when bad weather prevents the employees from doing other work."

(Weathers, *French Market-Gardening*, 1909, 38)

you can build a hotbed any time. I have built and directly seeded hotbeds in every month of winter with success.

Q: Can I make a small hotbed?

Yes. A hotbed the width of a shovel may not heat as well as a hotbed that is three feet by one foot, for example, but it will still work.

Q: Can I just buy a cold frame?

Yes. Cold frames (which are the same lids you use for hotbeds) are available online from many gardening sources and can be found in most garden supply catalogs. But there are a couple of drawbacks. Expect to pay between one hundred and two hundred dollars for a single cold frame. And more important,

commercial cold frames are simply too tall. As explained earlier, the best success for deep-winter gardening with a cold frame or hotbed comes when the frame is close to the earth. The more above ground the frame is, the more heat it will lose during the night, putting your vegetables at risk of freezing. That said, I do have two cold frames that are each more than a foot above ground. I use them for mature Swiss chard and cabbages. For these large vegetables, the lids that hug the ground don't have enough space—and these large frames work well. I bought one of my frames online for about one hundred bucks. The other I built myself in January on my kitchen table out of wood scraps and scrap greenhouse plastic. The one I built is much sturdier than the purchased one, but even the purchased one has done well for several years.

Q: When building hotbeds, can I use the same holes year after year?

Yes. When spring arrives, I take the lids off my hotbeds and use them as regular garden beds for the summer. At the end of autumn, I dig the (roughly) year-old manure or leafy green material out of the hole. By now, this has turned into a rich compost, and I put it on the garden beds or even use it as the growing medium for the new hotbeds. Digging out the holes is easy because the now-composted manure is light and easy to move. Once the holes are empty, refill them with fresh green animal manure or leafy green material. But you don't have to refill them immediately—they can sit empty as needed.

Q: I live in a windy area. Will the lid of my cold frame or hotbed blow away?

Yes! No one lives with more winter wind than we do in Utah, and yes, early on I would find the lids to my beds blown all over the neighborhood. But I found a simple solution. First of all, the frame lids that hug the earth have never blown away at my house—it is only the larger frame lids that tend to take flight in a storm. For these, the trick that has worked perfectly for me is tying a brick at each end of a short piece of rope and then hanging the rope over the top of the cold frame or hotbed, weighed down by the bricks at each end. Since I started doing this, I have never had another "flier."

Q: Should I cover the hotbed with a blanket at night?

Some people do. I don't. Historically, hotbeds and cold frames were covered every night with woven straw mats. Today, people put blankets over beds at night. I have never done this, mostly because we have a simple rule at our house: children and pets must thrive on benign neglect, and the garden must do 98 percent of the work of growing the food. Both my wife and I work full-time. I have six step-daughters, and we have five grandchildren. I work a couple part-time teaching jobs, I write books, and we have a large garden. I also have thirty-five chickens, a horse, and two cows. Not to mention the dozens of book signings keeping me busy. So you can see why we have these rules. If I had to cover my hotbeds and cold frames each night and remove the coverings every morning, my entire winter garden would be dead

WHEN SPRING ARRIVES, I TAKE THE LIDS OFF MY HOTBEDS AND USE THEM AS REGULAR GARDEN BEDS FOR THE SUMMER.

from neglect. Luckily, our garden thrives in winter even though I've never once used a blanket or mat of any kind.

Q: Do I need to go out and sweep the snow off the hotbed or cold frame?

No! Snow and even ice on top of your garden frame lids acts as insulation or a blanket, holding in the heat. So leave the snow and ice where they are. If you need to open your frames to either water or harvest inside, and the snow or ice slides off, that is fine too. Don't worry about it. And many people are surprised to learn that frames covered in deep snow still get enough light, without any problems. Snow and ice actually spread the light, like prisms.

Q: My frame has thick dust on it. Should I wash it?

Naw. Dust collects on frame lids during the winter, sometimes by blowing wind and sometimes after rain and snow and frost.

Eventually another storm will come and clear away the worst of it. If it looks terrible to you or if you want to see inside the frame lid without opening the frame and exposing the vegetables to the cold, then use a handful of snow to wipe away the dust. Otherwise, don't worry about it.

Q: Is using manure in a hotbed safe? Can I still eat my vegetables?

If used correctly, manure is absolutely safe. The key is this: Your vegetables should never, ever come in direct contact with manure. Wait at least 90 days before harvesting above-ground vegetables from beds prepared with manure, and 180 days before harvesting any root crops from beds prepared with manure. Remember that when you are putting manure in a hotbed as a natural source of heat, you are always putting a three- to six-inch layer of soil or compost on top to plant in. Never plant directly in manure!

APPLES

Few people now remember that it is possible to have fresh backyard apples in winter—we are so used to buying apples in the grocery store. Interestingly, most of the apples in the grocery store are considered winter apples—the kind that store well and last for a long time. What this all means is that you can have fresh winter apples, without going to the grocery store, if you have space for a tree and know which variety to choose.

Keeping winter apples is not hard. Winter varieties are the last to ripen—as late as Halloween—and I simply pick mine fresh off the tree, put them in a bucket with a lid, and put them in the root cellar or garage. The apples actually stay fresh a little longer in the unheated garage, which is a little colder than the root cellar.

I should note that different kinds of winter apple varieties have different characteristics.

Some apples slowly become a little soft in storage. These are called baking apples, and they make great pie and apple crisp. Some, like "Keepsake" (see below), stay crisp and ready to eat out of your hand. Some are sweet, some are sharply tart, and some begin tart and become more mellow over time. Some might be mealy but are perfect for juice or cider. You'll want to do some research before choosing the perfect winter-keeper apple for you. Once you make the investment, you'll be rewarded with fresh apples for decades to come—even when the snow is flying outside.

RECOMMENDED VARIETIES FOR THE WINTER GARDEN

My hands-down favorite winter apple is Keepsake, which was the far-and-away winner of an apple taste test held by friends of mine. (An apple tasting party is a great way to spend an evening. We had a variety of

•APPLES•

"Winter apples will keep all the better for being left in an all open airy place as late as it is safe to do so. . . .

". . . The best apples of the season . . . were brought out of a milk vault [on] Feb 7, 1892. They were Fallawaters, of a rich yellow color, with characteristic shading. They were remarkable for size but more remarkable for their perfect preservation. Compared with apples kept in the cellar of the same house they were in far better order. The inference is that the deeper milk vault maintained a more uniform temperature. The vault had a small ventilator direct to the open air. The temperature as near as could be ascertained was about 33 [degrees]."

("Winter Apples," *Portland Guardian*, June 26, 1895)

Author's note: *Orangepippin.com has this to say about the Fallawater apple variety: "Good sauce and culinary apple. Large, green fruit turning to light green upon ripening. Sometimes over 6 inches in diameter. Subacid to mildly sweet flavor" ("Fallawater apple," Orange Pippin). Interestingly, they don't mention the storage ability of this variety.*

44

cheeses with ours, and we nibbled on crackers between varieties to help keep the flavor of each apple from influencing the next one.) After the tasting, I ordered a Keepsake apple tree with my friend Julie Peterson from Maple Valley Orchards. Orangepippin.com, a website that reviews historic apple varieties, says this about Keepsake: "Unattractive, irregularly shaped, 2.25 to 2.75 inch diameter, 90% red fruit. Fine grained, hard, very crisp, juicy light yellow flesh. Strongly aromatic flavor. Very hardy. Mellows with age. Attains peak fresh eating quality in January or February. Keeps in storage through April."[1] It is that last part that caught my eye—peak fresh eating in the coldest months of the year, and it stores until spring! I can vouch that this variety is indeed very crisp and, even better, very sweet—a truly great apple. The aroma is literally mouth-watering. I'm getting hungry just thinking about it. And I have to disagree that the apple is "unattractive"; it simply looks like an heirloom apple. We have six varieties of apple growing on our property, and only one comes close to Keepsake, which is why I ordered a tree!

Garden and food writer Steve Albert recommends storing winter apples just above freezing to keep them "fresh right through the winter and into spring."[2] He touts the following varieties (the notes are his; for in-depth information about these and many other varieties, visit the experts at orange-pippin.com).

Apples

Arkansas Black:

"good storage keeper."

Ashmead's Kernel:

"tart when tree ripe, mellows with storage."

Baldwin:

"good to store for winter eating."

Black Twig:

"grassy, intense flavor."

Braeburn:

"stores well for up to 12 months."

Brown Russet:

"very late harvest."

Cox's Orange Pippin':

"excellent flavor; . . . good keeper."

Enterprise:

"firm, sweet; keeps well."

Fuji:

"honey-like flavor; stores well."

Golden Russet:

"flavor rich and aromatic; . . . keeps well in storage."

Gold Rush:

"dessert quality; . . . best after storage."

Idared:

"tangy-tart flavor; . . . keeps well."

Melrose:

"mildly tart, aromatic; good for storage."

Mutsu (Crispin):

"crunchy, moderately sweet to tangy; . . . long storage life."

Rome Beauty (Red Rome):

"juicy, crisp, slightly tart; . . . holds until June."

Tydeman's Late Orange:

"full flavor around Christmas; excellent for storage."

Winesap:

"slightly fermented winey flavor; . . . stores into June."

Notes

1. "Keepsake apple," Orange Pippin Ltd.
2. Albert, "Winter or Late-Season Apple Varieties."

BEANS

To prolong beans into bitter temperatures, the backyard gardener has three options. The first is to put a cold frame over fall-planted beans when freezing weather arrives. This will prolong bean plants down to about twenty degrees, if the cold frame is kept as low to the plants as possible. The second option is to plant early winter beans from seed in a hotbed. This will keep beans alive down to about ten degrees or lower, especially if the frame is covered with a blanket on the coldest nights. The third option is to plant beans in January or February using a two- or three-foot-deep hotbed. (Keep in mind that where I live, we can't start beans until mid-May because of frost.) Even in April, I'd still use three feet of manure to heat the bed because beans will freeze and die at thirty degrees.

It may be counterintuitive, but I recommend growing pole beans in hotbeds, not bush beans. This is because pole beans, when they don't have a pole to support them, simply vine on the ground. This has two great advantages for the hotbed: First, the bean stalk will lie on the ground, where it will be much warmer at night and thus much less prone to freeze. Second, you can keep the pole bean, without a pole, under a low cover. And then, when all danger of frost is past, you can simply stick a pruned sucker branch in the ground from one of your fruit trees and tie up the vine—and suddenly, in late May, when everyone else's beans are just sprouting, your beans are beginning to flower. And you'll have the earliest beans you've ever eaten from your garden.

•BEANS•

"Although Haricot Beans are not now grown so extensively, as a forced crop [grown in a cold frame or hotbed], by gardeners near Paris as they were formerly, it may be worth while describing the process. . . .

"Although there are now many varieties of Dwarf Beans, those suitable for early or forced crops are somewhat restricted. Amongst the best for the purpose are: Early Dwarf Frame Haricot, which grows 6 to 7 in. high, is very early, and has green seeds. . . . The Early Black Belgian Haricot is a black-seeded variety, next in earliness to the first named, and a much stronger grower requiring more space. The Early Chalandray has yellow seeds; the Early Dwarf Étampes, a strong grower, with white seeds. . . . One variety with yellow seeds . . . is known as 'Six Weeks.' I have grown it in the open air in the usual way, and much to my astonishment I picked the first pod exactly six weeks after the seeds were sown.

". . . [After transplanting seedlings,] each young Bean plant is buried up to the seed-leaves in the soil; if this is inclined to dryness, a gentle watering must be given. . . .

". . . The first pods may be picked six, eight, or ten weeks after the seed has been sown."

(Weathers, *French Market-Gardening*, 1909, 89–91)

BEETS

Winter beets can be a bit tricky to plant. Simply overwintering the beets you planted in spring doesn't work well because beets get woody and tough as they age, and the larger the beet, the less likely it is to make it through winter. The hardiest and best-tasting winter beets are young, which means that you will need to plant your seed in early August. If you plant when it is too hot—late July, for example—the seed will not germinate as well. But the young beets need enough time to form a good root before the days shorten too much. So early August usually does the trick for sowing beet seed for winter eating.

HOW TO GROW AND HARVEST

Beets tend to grow very slowly at first and then form a root globe fairly rapidly, so you might check them one week in October and think they are never going to amount to anything for winter eating, and a week later they will have a root the diameter of a quarter. Cover the beets with a cold frame in late fall, before the ground begins to freeze. Harvest as needed throughout the winter. If you have a period in winter when the temperature is below freezing both night and day, your beets will eventually suffer damage from the freeze. To prevent this, you have a few options: stuff the cold frame with straw until temperatures rise above freezing again, cover the cold frame with a blanket, simply pick the young beets and put them in the crisper drawer of your fridge, or box them (see below).

BOXING BEETS

Some people prefer to box root vegetables for winter use, rather than storing them in the ground in the garden. There is an advantage to boxing beets—you won't have to go

Beets

Recommended Varieties for the Winter Garden
•BEETS•

Any variety of beet can be used for winter growing, but there are two varieties of beets that I prefer to grow any time of year: Albino and Chioggia.

Albino is an old sugar beet that is rare now, though you can get the seed from Baker Creek Seed Company. The beet is pure white and tastes very little like a beet because it is so sugary. When I take fresh Albino beets to my "Forgotten Skills" classes for tasting in winter or summer, the response is inevitably shock and awe—no one has ever tasted anything like it. And if you can keep yourself from eating them all, you can use them to make molasses sugar. You can read about how to do that in my first book.

Chioggia is an Italian heirloom beet that is simply one of the most beautiful things you can grow in a garden. When sliced open, Chioggia has a pattern of rings alternating bright red and pure white, and this pattern stays even when cooked. They have a bright, sweet flavor that is unlike any other beet. They don't bleed at all, unlike traditional beets. Try them!

For the record, I also have a least favorite beet—Ruby. This is just a weird variety. It tastes weird to me, and it certainly looks weird—the color is almost a fluorescent jewel-tone of red, and it looks fake, kind of like the strange, bright red dye that grocery store butchers spray on day-old hamburger to make it look fresh-ground. This beet would be great, however, for making a unique color of natural dye for wool or cotton, for example.

out into the winter weather in your backyard to get your winter beets. And you'll get fresh winter beet salad. More on that in a moment.

To box your beets, use a plastic storage box, or line a cardboard box with a plastic garbage bag. Fill with wet pine shavings (you can get them inexpensively at pet stores or farm supply stores). Take the mature beets from your late fall garden and trim the leafy greens an inch above the top of the root, but don't cut the top of the root. Put them in the box in layers, and cover the beets completely so that you can't even see them in the box. Then store the box in your unheated garage or root cellar in darkness through the winter, taking beets out as you want them.

TENDER WINTER BEET GREENS
("Nocturnal" or "Sleeping" Beet Greens)

There is another advantage to boxing your beets—you can grow beet salad greens.

When beets are boxed for winter storage, they will slowly begin to grow leaves in the dark. These leaves are tender and beautiful and are fantastic in salad. Even if you layer your beets three deep in a box, all the beets will grow these leaves above the top of the pine shavings—so be sure to leave room, and don't put a lid on the box or stack anything on top.

Interestingly, even in the dark, beet greens develop some red stems in the leaves, just as they do in the summer garden, and this makes them look even better in a fresh winter salad. Better yet, if you cut these naturally blanched leaves, they will quickly grow back. Best of all, the flavor of the beet will be unaffected, and you can still eat them like normal.

Knowledge from Historic Gardens and Gardeners
•CABBAGES•

"[In Paris] nice Cabbages in the early spring are always highly appreciated, and when in market early are almost sure to command good prices. . . .

"About the end of August, or early in September, seeds are sown, and these dates are very strictly adhered to. If sown much earlier or later the plants afterwards are inclined to run to seed instead of forming heads. . . .

". . . [After transplanting,] the young plants have the stems buried until the lower leaves rest on the surface of the soil. They are spaced out 18 in. to 2 ft. apart in shallow furrows about a foot apart.

"From the same batch of seedlings it is possible to arrange for two distinct crops. This is done by placing some of the plants on warm and sheltered borders that have been deeply dug and well manured. . . . Furrows 4 to 5 in. deep are drawn, and into these the Cabbages are planted. The soil thus drawn up in little ridges on each side of the shallow furrow serves to protect the "collar" of the young plant during the winter months. In the course of time the soil from the ridges gradually crumbles down, and, coming in contact with the plants, keeps them warmer than would otherwise be the case with plants on a perfectly level piece of ground."

(Weathers, *French Market-Gardening*, 1909, 92–94)

CABBAGE
ALSO BROCCOLI, CAULIFLOWER, BRUSSELS SPROUTS

Cabbages and all of the other brassica vegetables—broccoli, cauliflower, Brussels sprouts, kale, kohlrabi, chard, mustard greens, and spinach—have a sweet, crisp texture in the winter garden that is unlike anything else. And you can make so many great things to eat with them; using cabbage alone, you can make cabbage rolls, cabbage in soup, stir-fry, and the famous Russian borscht. But my favorite use for cabbage continues to be on sandwiches and in tacos. Simple, easy, delicious. I love the toothsome sweetness!

RECOMMENDED VARIETIES FOR THE WINTER GARDEN

Getting cabbage, broccoli, Brussels sprouts, or cauliflower to begin heading out in the fall before the ground freezes means transplanting in late summer. You can use any variety of broccoli, Brussels sprouts, or cauliflower. When it comes to cabbages, you will need to choose an early variety. I have listed some below, with descriptions from the companies that offer them. If you don't choose an early variety, then you will be overwintering later varieties to get cabbage early in spring, instead of fresh in winter. Beware, however, that some varieties overwintered in my garden have refused to head until the next fall—a year later. And some have simply produced small heads and then gone to seed. Early cabbage varieties were historically developed for the autumn garden to be eaten during winter. Here are some of those varieties:

❉ Coeur de Boeuf des Vertus: "French bull-heart type cabbage that has tall, pointed green heads that are early and quite tender."[1] Seed offered by Baker Creek Heirloom Seed Company (rareseeds.com).

❄ **Early Jersey Wakefield:** "70 days [on all vegetables, day count refers to days from transplant to maturity]. Introduced in the 1840s, with tasty 2-lb. sweet and flavorful conical heads. This very early variety was sold commercially by Peter Henderson in the late 1860s."[2] Seed offered by Baker Creek Heirloom Seed Company (rareseeds.com).

❄ **Tete Noire:** "This traditional French variety is very rare outside of Europe. Solid, deep-red heads are of good quality and are mostly grown as an autumn variety in France."[3] Seed offered by Baker Creek Heirloom Seed Company (rareseeds.com).

❄ **Golden Acre:** "A very early round headed cabbage often used for pack sales and forcing. Heads are ball shaped and can grow close to 5 pounds so size isn't sacrificed for earliness."[4] Seed offered by Pinetree Garden Seed (superseeds.com).

WHEN TO PLANT

All brassica vegetable seed can take two weeks to germinate and can be slower to grow in fall than in spring, which can make planting for the winter garden tricky. Plant seed in late July or the first week of August. For best success, start the seed indoors. It will be really hard to muster yourself to even think about winter, let alone start planting the winter garden, in the heat of July. But when the temperatures have begun to cool in late August, it may be too late for your cabbage to make a head before the ground freezes and growth all but comes to a halt. Cabbages and so on will grow in winter in a cold frame, but growth will be very slow, and the outer leaves will suffer some damage from the cold.

Notes

1. "Couer De Boeuf Des Vertus Cabbage," Baker Creek Heirloom Seed Co.

2. "Early Jersey Wakefield," Baker Creek Heirloom Seed Co.

3. "Tete Noire Cabbage," Baker Creek Heirloom Seed Co.

4. "Golden Acre Cabbage," Pinetree Garden Seeds.

CARROTS

Nothing tastes like a winter carrot—and today, a winter carrot is one of the rarest of all vegetables. They don't sell them in the grocery store, so you can only get them fresh out of your own backyard. And picking fresh winter carrots for your kitchen could not be easier!

RECOMMENDED VARIETIES FOR THE WINTER GARDEN

Any variety of carrot can be used for winter gardening if you follow the instructions on page 57. I regularly grow yellow, orange, red, white, and purple carrots. Some of my favorite varieties are Jaune Obtuse du Doubs, Berlicum, Amarillo, Nantes, Cosmic Purple, Danvers Half Long, St. Valery, and White Belgian. I do not grow any hybrid vegetables in my garden for reasons spelled out in my first book, so I have not tested hybrid carrots in the winter, but I know other people who have used them just fine.

One variety of carrot deserves special mention here. Parisienne is an old variety from France that was specifically developed for forcing in hotbeds during winter two centuries ago. Several forcing varieties existed, most of which are now extinct (for information about extinct vegetables, see the story of "Petite Noire" in the lettuce chapter of this book). Forcing carrots simply means growing them in winter under glass in hotbeds. This was a common practice in Europe and the United States before the invention of grocery stores and industrial food shipped long distances. French family farmers were famous for interplanting vegetables in winter so as not to waste any space or time in the hotbeds. Carrot seeds were planted with

•CARROTS•

"The Carrot is brought to great perfection in French gardens, and vast quantities of juicy, tender roots are grown year after year. The smaller-rooted varieties are preferred especially by intensive growers, as they are easily forced, are far superior to the larger kinds, and find a more ready sale not only in the central markets of Paris, but also in Covent Garden and other English markets. . . .

". . . Seeds of *Paris Forcing* or *Early Forcing Horn* are sown for the first crop during October, on finely prepared mould about 6 in. deep on the surface of the mild hot-bed. After sowing the seeds and slightly covering them with soil, they should be gently beaten down with a piece of flat board. Very often, if not always indeed, Radishes are sown at the same time, but before the Carrots and a little deeper. Germination takes place in about a fortnight, and from this time onwards air is given on all occasions when the weather is favourable, if only for half an hour or so each day. This prevents etiolation or yellowing, and encourages the proper development of the leaves and roots.

"In November, and again in December, sowings of the same varieties may be made on hot-beds about 18 in. thick."

(Weathers, *French Market-Gardening*, 1909, 99–100, 102)

56

winter lettuce and radishes. Today, very few people grow winter carrots anymore because carrots can be bought in grocery stores year-round. Grocery store carrots are stored in huge warehouses filled with carbon dioxide to keep out oxygen, which keeps them from rotting. This is why carrots in the grocery store are so dry and bland compared with fresh winter garden carrots.

THREE METHODS FOR GROWING WINTER CARROTS

1. Simple Winter Carrots

Although you can force carrots in winter (more on that in a moment), for the backyard gardener there is no need. The simplest way to get fresh carrots in winter is to not eat all your spring carrots.

How To Plant

Plant your carrots as normal in spring—just make sure you plant enough to feed your family through winter too. If you like to make winter soups, stews, and roasted vegetables as I do at my house, fresh carrots are going to be one of your most popular winter vegetables. My advice is to plant at least double what you think you will need—you will be surprised by how fast you can go through carrots in the winter.

As your spring-planted carrots mature, you will use them as needed, of course. In late autumn, you will need to cover the carrots you have left in the garden with a thick layer—about twelve inches—of yard leaves, straw, hay, or grass clippings. You can use leaves (or hay and so on) in bags, or you can just spread the stuff on the ground. Leaves not in bags might blow away in the wind. Hay or straw does not tend to blow away, in my experience. I prefer not to use bags because it is hard to get them close enough together to really cover the carrots completely.

Let me be clear—you don't do anything to the carrots but cover them. The carrots are not picked or pulled out of the ground. They are left exactly where they grew. Carrot tops will withstand several hard frosts, so there is no need to cover them too soon. However you will need to cover them completely before the ground begins to freeze solid.

Especially when you cover garden carrots with a layer of mulch (leaves or straw and so on) for winter, mice and voles can be a problem—they can't resist crawling under that warm layer of mulch and munching on a winter feast that was supposed to be for your family. This can usually be solved by having a barn cat or covering your carrot bed with a fine wire mesh (available cheap at any farm supply store, often called rabbit wire) before you put down your mulch. Or you can just do what I do and plant extra. If you have a horse or cow or pig, they will happily eat any leftovers. If you are concerned that little critters might steal your winter harvest, try boxing your carrots (method three in this chapter).

How To Harvest

Go out on a sunny winter afternoon and use a shovel or pitchfork to pull back the straw or leaves covering your carrot bed. Once you get down to the ground, you will see that the ground is not frozen. The green leafy tops have withered, of course. Use a shovel or hand trowel to carefully dig up the

2. Forcing Carrots for Winter

If you have a small garden space, or if you just want to experiment, you can force winter carrots in a hotbed. For instructions on building a hotbed, see the hotbed chapter. One caution: If you are using animal manure (instead of chopped green leaves) as your heat source, you must not grow carrots (or any root vegetable) in direct contact with un-composted green animal manure. Make sure that your growing medium, usually

GROCERY STORE CARROTS ARE STORED IN HUGE WAREHOUSES FILLED WITH CARBON DIOXIDE TO KEEP OUT OXYGEN, WHICH KEEPS THEM FROM ROTTING.

58

carrots so you don't accidentally cut them in half or break them. Because it's winter, you don't want to have to come outside to get carrots every time you cook, so gather enough to last your family for a couple of weeks.

It's not unusual for the top of the carrot to be discolored or damaged if it was sticking out of the soil. Just cut off and discard the tops of any discolored carrots. The part of the carrot that was underground will be sugary sweet and crisp; these will quite possibly be the best carrots you have ever tasted!

Once you have your winter carrots in the house, wash and trim them and store them in your vegetable crisper drawer for up to a couple of weeks, just like carrots from the grocery store.

compost, is deep enough that your mature carrots will never touch the animal manure below.

For winter forcing, plant your carrot seed in your hotbed in August. You can plant later, but planting in August will give your carrots the maximum amount of time to grow before the real cold of winter starts in. You should not need to cover the hotbed with a lid until later—perhaps as late as October, depending on the weather. The fastest-growing forcing carrots are Parisienne or Tonda di Parigi. These are both short, fat, round carrots developed long ago for winter forcing in France.

3. Boxing Carrots for Winter

Some people prefer to box root vegetables for winter use, rather than storing them in the ground in the garden under mulch or forcing them. There are two advantages to boxing carrots. First, you won't have to go out into the winter weather in your backyard to get your winter carrots. Second, you likely won't have to worry about mice. To box your carrots, use a plastic storage box or line a cardboard box with a plastic garbage bag. Fill with wet pine shavings (available inexpensively at pet stores or farm supply stores) or damp sand. Pine shavings are easier to work with and not as heavy, and they can be composted in spring when you are done with them. Take the mature carrots from your garden and put them in the box. The carrots will store longest and best if you "plant" them in the box vertically, just like they grew in the garden. Trim the leafy greens just at the top of the root, but don't cut the top of the root. Cover the carrots completely, so that you can't even see them in the box. Then store the box in your unheated garage or root cellar in darkness through the winter, taking carrots out as you want them. They may begin to slowly grow leaves, but this generally does not affect the quality or taste of the root.

CHINESE CABBAGE

For a long time, I assumed Chinese cabbage was too tender to attempt in the winter garden. I was wrong. Discovering extra dwarf pak choi—my favorite kind of Chinese cabbage—in my winter garden was a happy accident. I've grown extra dwarf pak choi for several years now because it grows so fast; it is often ready to eat within a month. These miniature plants have a great shape, kind of like a vase, and there is something mesmerizing about the squat, fat stems and curly, glossy green leaves. This is one of those garden plants that looks delicious in the garden—like something out of a storybook.

Another reason why I enjoy this plant is because it matures so early that you can get pure seed without having to worry about pollen contamination from other varieties in the species. This vegetable is so delicate looking that I had always assumed it was something that could only be grown in late spring. But one summer, I was slow to harvest all the seed I had let develop and some fell onto my garden pathway. To my surprise, the seed sprouted that fall. I was happy to have this free crop—any time vegetables want to plant themselves, that is the best kind of gardening! I figured I'd eat them until they froze with the first frost. But the first frost didn't faze them, and neither did the next—nor the snow, nor bitter temperatures. In fact, what I left in the garden slowly went to seed and stayed green and tender and tasty into January, when they were finally killed by a chicken who escaped into the garden and scratched the plants to bits, trying to get at the seeds in the flowers the plants had grown. It turns out that I had a great winter vegetable under my nose for years—all I had needed to do was give it a shot at winter glory.

Chinese Cabbage

I'm sure other Chinese cabbage varieties will work too, especially the smaller varieties. Experiment for yourself. I am proud to be the first person to offer extra dwarf pak choi to the world as part of Seed Savers Exchange, an important nonprofit organization of backyard seed growers across the United States.

RECOMMENDED VARIETY FOR THE WINTER GARDEN

Extra dwarf pak choi is a relatively new variety of Chinese cabbage. Seed is available from Kitazawa Seed Company (kitazawa-seed.com).

WHEN TO PLANT & HOW TO GROW

Sow some seeds every few weeks beginning in August. Use a hotbed for sowing seeds in November through February.

Caleb Warnock

HERBS

What would the winter dinner table be without herbs? Herbs make food worthwhile! Winter soups, savory stews, roasted vegetables, pasta, roasted meats, homemade pizza—I'm getting hungry just thinking about them! None of these would be worth eating without herbs, and fresh herbs in winter make everything taste better.

Some perennial herbs last through early winter, even through Christmas, in the backyard without any protection at all: sage, winter savory, thyme, oregano, common chives, garlic chives, rosemary. These same herbs will stay fresh much longer, if not the entire winter, in cold frames or under cloches (bell jars). Normally, cloches are not my favorite way of winter gardening, as I explained in the cold frames chapter. But when it comes to herbs, they might be the best choice. The problem is that kitchen herb gardens can be

hard to cover with a cold frame—in my garden, all the herbs are not planted together. And even if they were, it would not be feasible to try and cover all of them with one cold frame. Not to mention that many herbs are huge by fall—especially the perennials. So this is a case when individual cloches can come in handy. If needed, you can prune back your herbs to fit and dry the pruned leaves in case you run out of fresh herbs (or dry them to give away as Christmas gifts).

Other herbs can be started early in a hotbed, so you can harvest fresh herbs far earlier in the season. In February, as I write this, I have winter savory in a hotbed that sprouted a week ago from seed. I saved my pennies to build a geothermal greenhouse, which is where I overwinter my stevia. And now, in February, I have basil growing that I sprouted in January. If you like eating Italian food like I do, you can't go long without basil! Basil is far too tender to grow even in hotbeds (I've tried), but it thrives in my geothermal greenhouse.

I feel like I've just scratched the surface when it comes to testing the possibilities for winter herbs, whether it be in a cold frame, hotbed, or greenhouse. And I certainly don't grow every herb (yet). So experiment on your own, and see what you can do. Every success will only make your winter eating that much more savory!

64

LEEKS

Leeks bring life to almost any winter dish with their savory flavor—think of them as a gentler version of their cousin, the onion. Leeks are traditionally planted in early spring in the cold zones of the United States, but they can be given a significant jump-start if they are grown in a hotbed over winter or planted in a hotbed in January. And the earlier you can get your vegetables to mature, the earlier you will be able to eat them, so the effort is worth it. Leeks planted in early winter or in January or February will grow only slowly, so even low hotbed frames will work fine. Like many vegetables in the winter garden, leeks will hit a growth spurt in late February, and by late March, your leeks are likely to be strong enough to survive on their own without a cover, which is good because they would soon grow too tall for a hotbed cover anyway, especially a low-lying

cover. Watch the leeks carefully in the transition from covered to no cover. Make sure to harden them off by opening the cover during the day for a week or so, and then choose a warmer night as their first night without a cover, preferably with no snow. Where I live on the benches of the Wasatch Mountains, my growing season is so short, ninety-two days, that it is impossible for me to bring leeks to maturity unless I plant them early in spring or overwinter them in a cold frame or hotbed after planting the seed in autumn. I should note that leeks and onions don't like the winter greenhouse; it gets too hot for them (on a sunny day in December, January, and February, the greenhouse can reach one hundred–plus degrees if the vents are not opened in the morning). They do much better when planted as seed in the backyard hotbed.

Knowledge from Historic Gardens and Gardeners
•LEEKS•

"The Leek constitutes an important crop in French as well as in English market-gardens, and it is probable that, so far as open-air culture is concerned, there is but little difference in methods employed on both sides of the Channel. . . .

". . . Whichever variety is chosen, the main object in view is to secure Leeks of medium size in the early days of June.

"Seeds are sown thickly in the latter half of December on a hot-bed about 15 in. deep. . . . To hasten germination, it is a good plan to soak the seeds in luke-warm water for about twelve hours—more or less—in advance. If the primary root in the seed begins to show, it may be taken for granted that the seeds have soaked long enough."

(Weathers, *French Market-Gardening*, 1909, 139–140)

RECOMMENDED VARIETIES FOR THE WINTER GARDEN

Belgian Breeder's Winter Mix is a great winter leek. This seed is sold in the United States only by Wild Garden Seeds. This leek is hardy enough that, when planted in the fall, it will live all winter outside unprotected in the open garden, but it grows only extremely slowly in these conditions. It will mature a little faster if kept in a cold frame or hotbed. If seeded in fall, don't be alarmed if the seed takes even five or six weeks to sprout. They will sprout faster if planted in January in a hotbed, but they could still take three to four weeks, depending on the weather. I admit that I have not tried soaking them to hasten germination, as is recommended by the seed company.

Blue Solaise leeks have also worked well for me in the winter garden. I plant these in the hotbeds in January, and by mid-February they are happy and growing. These can also be planted in the fall or early winter.

There are probably other leek varieties that would work in the winter garden too, especially if grown in hotbeds. In fact, any variety of leek is likely to work in a hotbed. The two mentioned above are the ones I grow, but you could trial your own varieties.

67

Knowledge from Historic Gardens and Gardeners

•LETTUCE•

"The winter growing of lettuce is not yet practiced in Utah. There is a good demand for lettuce in Salt Lake City, Ogden, and in some of the smaller towns during the winter, but this demand is supplied by the California grown product. It is yet to be determined whether or not lettuce can be grown profitably under glass in this State. The recent high prices of the winter product indicate that the forcing of a moderate amount of lettuce can be done with profit.

"In the season of 1899–1900, the Experiment Station began a series of experiments with lettuce in the forcing house. The facilities for this work were very meager, only one bed five feet by fourteen feet in the center oft a small three-quarter span house being available. The work has now been continued two seasons and four crops have been grown."

For this winter lettuce trial, the first seed of Grand Rapids lettuce was sown on October 28, 1899. The first crop matured in ten weeks and was cut on February 1, 1900. A second crop was sown on January 16, 1900, and a bushel of composted manure was added to the forcing house soil. These lettuces had two to three leaves on February 14, and in nine weeks they had matured. A third crop was sown on November 21, 1900, and in ten weeks and two days it was mature and cut. According to measurements, the Grand Rapids was 60 percent heavier than the other lettuce tested, called Denver Market. The researchers reported that "Grand Rapids lettuce will be preferable to Denver Market on account of heavier yield, more attractive plants and less liability to tipburn and rot."

(Close, "Bulletin No. 76," 119, 121–125)

LETTUCE

I am passionate about winter lettuce. There is nothing like it.

I cut fresh lettuce out of my backyard garden all winter, even when the temperatures have been consistently as low as minus seventeen degrees Fahrenheit. You read that right!

The day you really begin to feel self-sufficient is the day in the dead-winter cold of January when you run outside and cut a fresh salad of gourmet lettuces from your backyard garden. People have been doing this for centuries—and it's much easier than you might think. And you should know that I am not gardening in Hawaii—if only! Like I said before, I live on the Wasatch Mountain bench in Utah, above five thousand feet. The average summer growing season in my city is the shortest in my county: just 92 days on average. If you are a gardener, you will know that this growing season is tiny. Most people have at least 120 days, if not more. And our winters are bitter and harsh. We get prolonged howling winds of up to one hundred miles an hour. We get repeated nights where the temperature dips to twenty below zero—so cold that you have to leave the faucets in the house running all night to keep the pipes from breaking. Every winter we get a four- to six-week stretch where the temperature does not rise above freezing ever, night or day.

Most people think the idea of fresh, backyard winter lettuce is laughable—or delusional. But they are wrong. And to prove it, I've had hundreds of people tour our garden, taste my winter lettuces, and take photos; I even sell them the winter lettuce seed I grow myself every year.

69

Lettuce

In the sixteenth, seventeenth, and eighteenth centuries, fresh winter lettuce—no matter how frigid and miserable the winter—was an everyday way of life. In fact, thousands if not tens of thousands of families made their living growing winter lettuce and other vegetables for the residents of Paris, London, and New York City on small farms surrounding those huge capitals.

You can grow fresh lettuce in winter in your backyard too. It's simple and easy.

RECOMMENDED VARIETIES FOR THE WINTER GARDEN
(ranked by preference)

1 Parris Island Cos romaine is my hands-down favorite. Without any protection in the open garden soil in the dead of winter, this will be one of the last lettuces to die back and become unusable. It resists hard frost almost completely and does not begin to die until after the ground has been frozen for several days. Even when it dies back, it is slow to die completely and will begin to grow new leaves if daytime temperatures rise into the high twenties, and it will grow relatively quickly (for a winter garden plant, which never grow as fast as summer garden plants) in temperatures above freezing.

I should note that I never buy seed for Parris Island Cos romaine because I harvest my own seed from plants grown in winter year after year, and therefore my personal variety has become more cold hardy over time than commercial varieties that have not been grown in winter. Because I believe my personal seed has in fact become more winter hardy than any seed on the market, I have renamed it Winter Green Jewel romaine, and I sell it under that name as available.

In a cold frame, the crisp, crunchy leaves stand up extremely well to the most bitter temperatures. This light green lettuce will also grow back if cut off at ground level, and it produces a large amount in a small space thanks to its upright habit and dense leaves.

This lettuce tastes great whether you eat it young or fully grown, and it is equally delicious in salads and on sandwiches, tacos, and more. When picked fresh from the winter garden, it will stay fresh for up to two weeks on the counter in a covered bowl with a little water in the bottom, or in the fridge in a covered bowl or plastic food bag with a little water to keep humidity high. This lettuce is also the easiest to clean, which makes it a valuable winter variety.

2 Green oak leaf is the single hardiest variety of all the winter lettuces, which is surprising because this is also one of the most delicate lettuces in any garden in any season. This variety is exceptionally hardy both in a cold frame and even in the open garden with no protection.

In a cold frame, green oak leaf will suffer less damage and grow faster, as will any winter lettuce variety. In open winter soil without protection of any kind, this lettuce withstands extremely cold temperatures, prolonged exposure to hard frost, and direct and prolonged contact with snow better than any other variety of lettuce, including Parris Island Cos.

Without the protection of a cold frame, this variety is the slowest to die back in prolonged and bitter cold and is the first to recover and grow new leaves if the temperature warms even slightly toward thirty-two degrees Fahrenheit.

Oak leaf will grow back if cut off at ground level. The flavor and texture is quite delicate, making this lettuce best suited for salads. Because the leaves are so beautiful, they are especially suited for mixing with other lettuce varieties in salad.

The only problem with this variety is that it is hard to clean, whether grown in or out of a cold frame. In winter, for reasons I have not been able to understand, a few random leaves within a head of this loose-type of lettuce die and must be removed before eating. This lettuce is also hard to clean because of the deep ruffling of the leaves and intricate growth habit. The dead leaves can be difficult to remove. I have not yet trialed oak leaf varieties in other colors in the winter garden, but they would be worth trying.

Grand Rapids lettuce won a winter garden cold frame trial conducted in a glass cold frame in 1899 by the Utah State University Extension Service, the only such winter lettuce trial that I know of in the United States In my garden, this does extremely well in a hotbed, even growing from seed planted in November or December! This variety will also last all winter in the garden without any protection at all, but it suffers from tip burn on the leaves and tends to become limp (but not dead) if bitter temperatures persist. So it tastes best when in a cold frame or hotbed. This lettuce, which is actually an old winter

variety from France, is called Grand Rapids because it grows so fast when forced (grown in a cold frame or hotbed) in winter. In my winter garden, this lettuce grows slowly but steadily all winter when planted from seed in October or November—and then in February, it suddenly begins to grow an inch a week, living up to its name. It is an amazing thing to see. When planted in late autumn and covered in a cold frame, this lettuce also grows four times faster than any other lettuce in my garden. In 1897, Grand Rapids was one of seven lettuce varieties sold in the Sears, Roebuck and Company catalog, and it was the only lettuce listed as a "forcing" variety. The price was twenty cents for four ounces.[1]

4 Winter Density lettuce is among the best lettuces for use in a winter cold frame because it is so hardy. Without protection, it will last a long time but will begin to die back once the ground freezes solid. For best eating over the whole winter, cover this lettuce (and all winter lettuces) with a cold frame in late autumn. The leaves are thicker than other loose-leaf lettuce types, and they can have hints of spinach flavor in taste and texture. One of the drawbacks of Winter Density is that it is not a dense or large plant, so you don't get as much out of this variety.

5 Tom Thumb lettuce is a beautiful, hardy winter lettuce variety which tastes great and performs well in a cold frame. This is actually another old French lettuce.

6 Merveille des Quatre Saison (Marvel of Four Seasons) is certainly one of the most beautiful winter lettuces you will ever see. In autumn and early winter, this lettuce is a spectacular mix of greens, reds, and bronzes. When hard frosts hit, this lettuce turns almost entirely deep burgundy red.

Unfortunately, this variety begins to die back quickly once the ground freezes solid. However, it performs excellently all winter when under a cold frame.

7 Brown Goldring is a rare variety that is breathtakingly beautiful in spring, fall, and early winter—so elegant that it is hard to make yourself pick it. It is also delicious (I picked it eventually). This butterhead resists hard frosts, but I have not had time to fully test it through deep winter yet. But I will, and I will eventually report my findings on my blog, calebwarnock.blogspot.com.

8 Caleb's Deep Winter—okay, the name is indulgent, but hear me out. In 2010, I became the only gardener in the United States to be a volunteer test grower of winter lettuce varieties for the federal government's germplasm program. The federal seed bank provided me with ten previously untested lettuce seed samples gathered from around the world. The results of the trial are still preliminary at this writing, but there is a clear winner. Because of my original research, I will get to name this seed and become the first person to sell it. So I'm thinking of naming it "Caleb's Deep Winter" because all ten varieties were grown over winter (planted as seed on October 1) without any protection to prove their worthiness and because I am the only one doing this kind of volunteer research in the United States

WHEN TO PLANT

August is a critical month for planting winter lettuces. Remember, because the number of sunlight hours is slowly waning, the growth rate of plants is beginning to slow down in August. To have enough quantity of lettuce to eat through December, January, and February, you need to plant in early to mid-August so that your plants have time to grow big before the ground freezes solid in December or January. One of the hardest parts of winter gardening is convincing yourself in August that you need to plant for winter. But it's critical to do it in August. Starting roughly in mid-November, the daylight hours are going to become so short and the temperature is going to begin to be so cold, that your winter garden plants will grow only slowly. So the lettuce you will eat in deep winter does most of its growing in September and October. When you harvest this lettuce over the winter, you can cut it at ground level, and it will begin to grow again very slowly. This growth will not begin to speed up until mid-February and March.

If you plant in September or October, you can still eat winter lettuce, but you will have to eat it as "baby lettuce," which means the plants will be small, so you will need to plant a lot more than you would have planted in August. In November, you can plant lettuce from seed in a hotbed. This lettuce will begin to sprout within a week, but it will grow in slow motion. If you plant during the first week of November, by the end of November your lettuce will be two little leaves. As I write this, it is mid-January, and the lettuce I planted in early November is now about the size of a quarter, with three small leaves on each plant. This lettuce is just now beginning to think about growing, and it will be ready to eat as baby lettuce in early March. From that point, it can be cut at ground level, and it will grow again and again, fairly rapidly, because spring will have arrived. By mid-March, you will be able leave the glass or plastic lid off the hotbed completely because this lettuce will need no further protection.

I recommend you try planting cold frame and hotbed lettuces every month throughout the winter, even just a little, so that you can experiment with what is possible in your area. Plus there is really something humbling and wonderful about going outside in the dead winter of December and January and lifting the lid of your hotbed to check on your tiny lettuce sprouts. And your gardening friends will be gobsmacked when you take them out to show them—and that is always fun!

HOW TO GROW

When I teach "Forgotten Skills" classes on winter gardening, I always give this advice: plant at least four times more winter lettuce than you think you will need. Winter lettuce will be much more popular with your family than you might think, and every year, no matter how much I plant, I seem to find myself wishing I had planted more—after all, if you run out in December or January, you can't quickly grow more.

All winter lettuce planted in August or September should be planted in an open, unprotected garden but in a spot where you can cover it with a cold frame later. You generally

Caleb Warnock

don't need to put a cold frame over the lettuce until sometime in October, depending on when you get prolonged hard frosts in your area. Lettuces seem to do best in my garden when the cold frame or hotbed lid is set just over the lettuce so there are little cracks or gaps where air can still go in and out all winter. Once bitter cold, prolonged deep freezes set in, you might think you need to push soil around the cold frame to seal every little crack, but this is not necessary in my experience—not with cold frames or hotbeds, using the lettuce varieties I have listed in this book.

Once you cover the lettuce, you will need to open the cold frame roughly every three weeks to water by hand. One caution: When your lettuce suddenly begins to look like it is dying in the cold frame or hotbed in November, December, January, or February, it is easy to think, "Well, Caleb was wrong. This lettuce can't survive the cold after all." But your lettuce is probably not dying of cold—it desperately needs a drink. Even in December and January, a cold frame or hotbed can get fairly warm during the day and sometimes even downright hot. And that means your lettuce is drying out slowly from the heat, even when the whole world seems to be frozen solid outside. So if your lettuce looks like it is dying, go water it, and it will quickly revive and look great. You don't need to water every week. I find that watering about every three weeks is okay, but you have to keep an eye on your cold frames and hotbeds, and if it becomes unusually warm, water them every two weeks. Water between noon and 3 p.m.

I have tried to be as detailed as possible in this chapter, but I don't want you, dear reader, to think this is intimidating or hard stuff. Growing fresh lettuce all winter in your backyard garden is easy and takes little time or effort. Anyone can do it, and kids love to help. No excuses. Everyone with even the smallest garden space should have fresh lettuce all winter. It is so much cheaper than the grocery store lettuce, and it tastes so much better! Be proud to feed your family fresh, healthy gourmet salads from your provident winter garden. And best of all, you will be teaching your children, young or old, at the dinner table about the bounty of the winter garden.

HOW TO HARVEST

Simply cut your lettuce off at ground level. You will need to do some cleaning. There will be a few dead leaves on your winter lettuce and a few winter-burned leaf tips. Pick these out to put in your compost later. After picking out the dead leaves, I wash my lettuce three times in a colander. If you are going to use the lettuce that day, you can put it on the counter in a covered bowl with just a splash of water in the bottom. This keeps the humidity high in the bowl, which is the key to keeping your lettuce fresh and crisp (whether you are picking it in winter or summer).

To make life easier in winter—after all, it's cold outside, and no one wants to go out and pick lettuce in a blizzard—I pick about a week's worth of lettuce at a time on a sunny winter afternoon. I keep it in a covered bowl, with a splash of water in the bottom, inside the fridge. It will stay fresh and crisp for up to two weeks, in my experience—far longer than anything you get from the grocery store. But make sure you clean it first before storing it, otherwise the whole batch will go bad within a day or two.

PETITE NOIRE: Lost Lettuce— The Story of the World's Most Important Lettuce, Now Extinct

As I said at the beginning of this chapter, I am passionate about winter lettuce. You might even say I'm obsessive.

And sad. Here's why. Earlier in this book, and in my first book, I reported a frightening fact: 96 percent of the vegetable varieties that were available in 1903 are now extinct.[2] Read that twice and let it sink in.

This is the story of one of those extinct vegetables.

Centuries ago, Petite Noire was the most important lettuce in France, the very best of all winter lettuces. It was beloved because it thrived in winter under cloches and needed little or no air circulation. That was a huge advantage because to grow other kinds of winter lettuces, gardeners had to regularly go out and open the glass bell jars to let in fresh air or else the lettuce did not grow well. That was a lot of work, and Petite Noire was a godsend.

Petite Noire did not exist by accident—it was bred, like all modern vegetables, by families of gardeners who improved it over centuries by saving the best seed from year to year to year, culling out unwanted traits and keeping the best traits. This is how all of our modern vegetables came to exist. Carrots, lettuce, beets, potatoes—none of them are found in the wild in the form that we now eat them on our dinner tables. The wonderful, delicious vegetables, fruits, grains, and even meat from animals we eat today took centuries of work and sacrifice to make what they are today.

And now, 96 percent of those garden foods are gone.

Of all vegetables, lettuce has suffered the most staggering loss. I could list many dozens if not hundreds of extinct lettuce varieties. I have spent hundreds of hours pouring over historic documents in English, French, and German to research historic lettuce—I know, it's crazy, but I became obsessed. I have spent a lot of time and money trying to find one lettuce variety in particular: Petite Noire.

But it is gone.

In the 1600s and 1700s, Petite Noire was a winter mainstay on thousands of family farms around Paris. I have documented that the seed arrived in America and was grown here as late as the 1800s. Over time this lettuce—as with all vegetables that were passed around Europe and eventually made their way to the United States—became known by different names, and I have been able to document some of them.

But I have not been able to find a single seed of Petite Noire. Not in this country nor in Europe. I have traced dozens of records to dead ends. I have consulted with historic garden experts from Mount Vernon and Seed Savers Exchange. I have searched the inventory records of seed banks in the United States, Europe, and Russia. I have slogged through documents and websites written in French and German. I have sought help from the largest online gardening forums in the United States and France. I have done everything I could think to do until there was nothing more to do.

I haven't given up hope. I like to think that somewhere in the antique French countryside, an old man or woman, perhaps the great-great-grandchild of one of those old French winter vegetable farm families— they were called *maraîchère*—is still planting Petite Noire and has kept it alive. All we have to do is find them.

In the meantime, it's worth noting the reason why so many vegetables have become extinct. Until World War II, most families

KNOWLEDGE FROM HISTORIC GARDENS AND GARDENERS

"The native country of the Lettuce is unknown. . . . According to Herodotus, it was in use 550 years before Christ; yet Pliny says the ancient Romans knew but one sort. In his time it was cultivated so as to be had at all times of the year. . . . In the privy-purse expenses of Henry VIII, in 1530, is mention of a reward to the gardener of York Place for bringing 'Lettuze' and cherries to Hampton Court. Gerarde, in his Herbal, 1597, gives an account of eight sorts cultivated in his day. . . . For early [winter] use, the 'Curled Simpson' and 'Black-seeded Simpson.' . . . Hundreds of acres of glass are devoted to the forcing of Lettuce in the United States. The variety used mostly for that purpose is known as 'Boston Market.' "

(Henderson, *Henderson's Handbook*, 215)

still grew at least some of their own food in their backyard. Those families, our not-so-distance ancestors, knew how to save pure seed and how to grow fresh food in winter. But the world changed. Grocery stores replaced family gardens, and those stores quickly began getting their food from industrial farms, not local families. Industrial farms grew only vegetables that would ship well and not rot on store shelves. And a new thing called "hybrid" seed came along, invented in the 1920s. It wasn't long until common wisdom held that hybrid seed—created by artificial pollination with secret breeding lines, often patented—was the only valuable kind of seed. The old kind of seed—the open-pollinated seed that had been grown for thousands of years—was outmoded, outdated, ridiculous. Hybrid seed was smart, new technology, the cutting edge of science. No one planted open-pollinated heirloom seeds much anymore, let alone a family garden. Not long after, getting food from the grocery store instead of the family garden became the norm; frozen food followed. Fast food was next. The nation stopped growing and saving backyard garden seed—there was no need.

Now, few people even know how to save pure seed. There is perhaps only a handful of gardeners left in the nation working to improve heirloom seed. I am one of them.

The only way to see Petite Noire lettuce today is in drawings published in books almost two centuries ago. Those drawings are all that remain of the lettuce that kept Paris from starving in winter.

What if, one day—perhaps if the economy were shaky at best, if the industrial food supply was increasingly contaminated, and if gas prices were jumping and food prices too—we needed to go back to the old way, the self-provident way, the twelve-month fresh family garden?

Notes

1. *1897 Sears Roebuck & Co. Catalogue,* 25

2. Center for Biodiversity and Conservation, "Biodiversity and Your Food."

Caleb Warnock

MANGELS

Most people have never heard of mangels, which are also called field beets or fodder beets and sometimes mangelwurzel or mangold. These huge beets are what homesteaders fed their livestock during winter for centuries before the invention of baled hay and mass-produced grain. I feed them to my horse and two cows. (I would feed them to my pig, if only my wife would let me have a pig. She has some kind of weird thing about pigs. But I love her anyway.) Mangels make excellent animal feed, and the livestock like them. The chickens like them. Even the mice and voles eat them right out of the garden soil in the dead of winter. Barnyard animals will also relish just about any root vegetable from your garden, summer or winter—beets, turnips, and carrots, for starters. The advantage of mangels is that they are extremely hardy, they grow to be huge—up to twenty pounds each—and they will be one of the very last vegetables to die back in the winter garden. In the 1825 book *An Encyclopedia of Agriculture*, John Claudius Loudon says field beets "appear to afford more nourishment than either turnips, carrots, or parsneps."[1]

If picked before they freeze, mangels store very well. If left out in the frozen garden without protection, you can pull them straight from the ground and feed them to the animals. And you will be surprised how quickly barnyard animals that have never seen a mangel in their life will take to eating these old-time roots. I am told that people eat them too, when the mangels are very young and tender. But when they are mature, they are woody and fibrous and not anything you would want to serve at the dinner table.

Knowledge from Historic Gardens and Gardeners
•MANGELS•

"The field-beet, commonly called the mangold-wurzel and sometimes erroneously the root of scarcity . . . has been a good deal cultivated in Germany and Switzerland, both for its leaves and roots; the leaves are either used as spinach or given to cattle; and the roots are either given to cattle, used in distillation, or in the manufacture of sugar. . . .

"Any soil will suit this plant provided it is rich: immense crops have been raised on strong clays; but such soils are not easily prepared for this sort of crop, and are also ill adapted for after-culture. . . .

"The application of the field-beet is almost confined to the fattening of stock, and feeding of [milk] cows. Near London they are in repute for the latter purpose; and, according to [Professor] Von Thaer, they cause a great increase of milk, as well as improve its flavour. The tops are first taken off, and given by themselves; and then the roots are taken up, washed, and given raw."

(Loudon, *An Encyclopedia of Agriculture*, 866)

our small farm as one of those that is now bringing this tradition back. I figure the more we can do to be self-sufficient not only in feeding ourselves but in feeding our barnyard animals, the better off we will be. And the financial benefits are immediate and obvious—hay and grain have become expensive. Fodder beets are practically free.

OTHER MANGELS

Mammoth Red Mangel beet: "100 days. Huge, up to 20 lbs. each, large yields per acre. Highly used for livestock feed in the 1800's. Or picked small for table use."[3]

Geante Blanche beet: "A 'Giant White' fodder beet that is a mainstay in France as a beet for livestock. Long, pointed white roots with a green collar are sweet and keep well for winter use."[4]

Yellow Cylindrical beet: "Very large, oblong golden-yellow mangel beets are sweet and tasty if picked small, or let them mature for high-quality stock feed. A rare European heirloom that can grow huge, it also makes tasty greens."[5]

WHEN TO PLANT & HOW TO GROW

To get mangels to their huge size, plant them in spring at the same time you plant garden beets. These are heavy feeders and will need a good dose of manure or frequent compost tea applications to reach their top size. When you want to feed them to your

RECOMMENDED VARIETIES FOR THE WINTER GARDEN

One downside of mangels is that they have become extremely rare, and seed can be difficult to find. Many mangel varieties that were historically grown on small farms are now extinct. I grow Giant Yellow Eckendorf from Baker Creek Heirloom Seed Company.

This is how they describe this beet: "These big yellow-skinned roots are perfect for growing as animal food, a tradition that is finally being brought back on many small farms."[2] I am happy to say that you can count

barnyard animals, pull the mangels up and give them to the animals root, leaves, and all. My horse takes them right out of my hand, like an apple!

Notes

1. Loudon, *An Encyclopedia of Agriculture*, 866.

2. "Giant Yellow Eckendorf Beet," Baker Creek Heirloom Seed Co.

3. "Mammoth Red Mangel Beet," Baker Creek Heirloom Seed Co.

4. "Geante Blanche Beet," Baker Creek Heirloom Seed Co.

5. "Yellow Cylindrical Beet," Baker Creek Heirloom Seed Co.

Caleb Warnock

MELONS

Yes, you can grow melons in winter! One of the most astonishing things I learned when reading the oldest gardening books I could get my hands on is that melons have been routinely grown in winter for centuries. Fresh melon in winter? Sign me up!

RECOMMENDED VARIETIES FOR THE WINTER GARDEN

Of the melon varieties that were successfully grown in winter centuries ago, I have only been able to find seed for two: Noir des Carmes cantaloupe and Prescott Fond Blanc cantaloupe.

Noir des Carmes cantaloupe has changed my garden forever. I have trialed at least forty kinds of melons, and to this day Noir des Carmes is the only melon I have been able to get to thrive and grow in abundance in my extremely short growing season. I also have this strange dislike of growing melons on black plastic, and Noir des Carmes grows perfectly without any plastic. Little did I know, however, that this melon was also the premier winter-growing melon for centuries! I almost fell out of my chair when I read that for the first time in one of my old winter gardening books. Here is a melon I grow and love—and it is the best for winter!

In a trial in my garden, Prescott Fond Blanc did not perform as well as Noir des Carmes, so I no longer grow it.

HOW TO PLANT & GROW

Getting melons to take hold in my winter garden has been a learning curve. Noir des Carmes withstands the cold better than any other melon, but it is still tender and must have the heat of a hotbed—a deep hotbed. In fact, it needs a three-foot-deep hotbed. I have tried this melon in a hotbed heated by only a foot of manure—the same kind of hotbed where I can get winter lettuces, cucumbers, mustards, collards, and much more to sprout. And the Noir des Carmes will sprout—but only slowly. The real problem comes after the melon has sprouted; a bitter night, which means anything below ten degrees, freezes Noir des Carmes after a few nights and kills it.

At first, this freezing was frustrating. So I went back to the old books and discovered I'd missed one crucial piece of information.

started again. And the mice ate the sprouts again.

I was not happy, to put it mildly. I went back to the oldest gardening books I could find and read carefully to find out how these authors dealt with mice. They practically buried their hotbed frames in hot manure—all the way around the sides, all the way up to the glass. Apparently using this much hot manure to surround the outside of the frame kept the mice at bay while sealing in the heat from the manure underneath the plants inside. By the time I discovered this information through my research, it was too late for me to start again in time to get information

MY RECOMMENDATION IS THAT YOU REMOVE THE COVER ONLY FOR A MOMENT AT A TIME TO CHECK ON THEM, AND ONLY ON THE WARMEST SUNNIEST DAYS.

The hotbeds have to be heated with three feet of manure below the ground. Melons need a lot of heat to ward off the killing cold. So I had to start over.

This was my first winter trying melons in a hotbed heated by three feet of fresh manure. For a while, it worked great, and I expected to have fresh cantaloupe in April or May at the latest. And then one day, I went out into the winter garden to discover the mice had burrowed into my hotbed—and they had eaten every cantaloupe plant down to the ground, leaving behind only their tunnels. (I know it was mice because the tunnels were small, not the size of vole tunnels). So I

into this book. I will try again this winter and put the results on my blog. One thing I know for sure—if they could get ripe cantaloupe in early spring three hundred years ago, I am going to get ripe cantaloupe in early spring too. I'm determined.

Melons that you want to plant in the backyard hotbed can be jump-started if you sprout them in a sunny window in the house—however, they need to be moved into the hotbed the very moment they start to sprout. Don't wait until they have fully sprouted. I don't know why, but they do better if you move them outside once they have just begun to break the soil, before the first leaves, called cotyledons, have even opened. They acclimatize better outside. If you are going to transplant a melon sprout from the house, wait at least three or four days after you have created your new hotbed. The manure will need a few days to begin decomposing underground and warm up. The melon sprout will do better if the compost is fully active.

You can plant the seed directly in the hotbed. If you do this, don't be surprised if it sprouts slowly. You many not see any movement for two or three weeks, depending on the weather. (Melons sprout faster in winter if there are sunny days. They will take longer if the weather has been cloudy.)

Take caution: many winter garden fruits and vegetables love to have the cover removed on a sunny, warm winter day when temperatures are in the forties or fifties. And many don't need any cover at all, day or night, beginning in mid-April. But cantaloupes do not fall in this group. My recommendation is that you remove the cover only for a moment at a time to check on them, and only on the warmest, sunniest days. And never, ever keep them uncovered until you are sure all danger of frost has passed—imagine working to nurture a hotbed cantaloupe only to have it freeze in a rogue May frost.

You won't have luck planting melons before January. Like many winter plants, melons do best if sprouted after the winter solstice. For more information on why the winter solstice affects plants, see page 20.

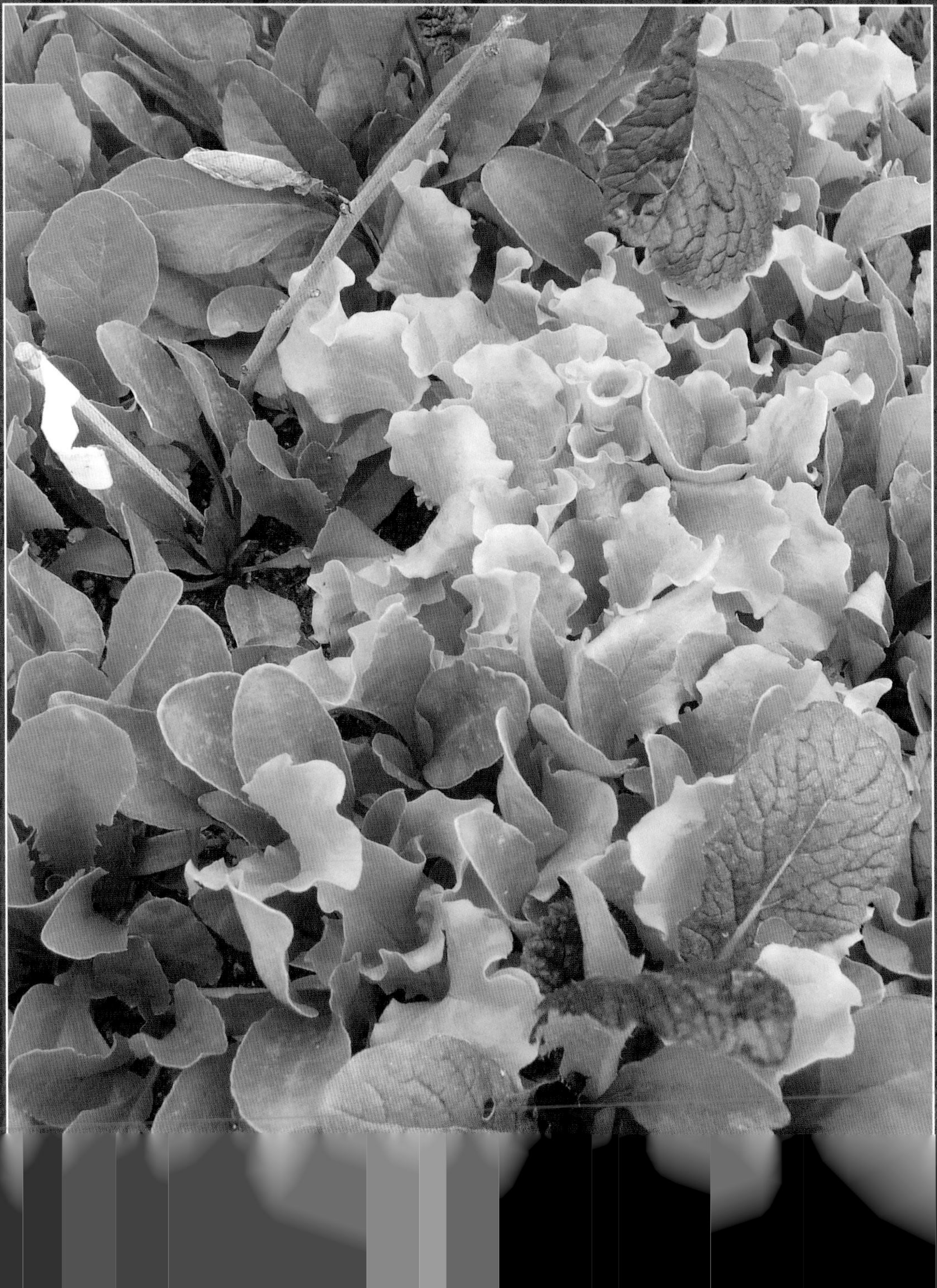

MUSTARD GREENS

RECOMMENDED VARIETY FOR THE WINTER GARDEN

I use Osaka Purple mustard, which has fantastic rounded, deep purple leaves with green stems and some green on the leaves. These are striking in the garden and even more striking in the snow. They have a sharp taste that works well when added to salads and omelets. If they are steamed or sautéed, the sharp taste disappears.

WHEN TO PLANT & HOW TO GROW

Osaka Purple grows rapidly—the baby greens can be ready to eat in three weeks. And this plant is hardy against frost and lasts a surprisingly long time in the open garden with no protection at all. To have this plant all winter long, protect it with a cold frame or grow in late fall in a hotbed.

·ONIONS·

"Although there are many varieties of Onion in cultivation, there is now only one specially adapted for intensive cultivation as practised by the Parisians market-gardeners, that is, the variety known as 'Blanc hâtif de Paris' or 'Early White Paris.' Formerly another variety, the 'Jaune des Vertus,' was extensively cultivated, but has been discarded as it is not sufficiently remunerative.

"Seeds are sown in beds about the middle of August. . . .

". . . These blanc hâtif or 'Early White Onions' are at first planted very thickly by market-gardeners, who allow little more than 1 or 1½ in. between them. . . . They are not allowed to reach their full size, but are sold as soon as the bulbs are an appreciable size. In this way the Onions are cleared as quickly as possible and the soil becomes available for another crop. . . .

"Many growers also sow seeds of the 'Early White' (blanc hâtif) Onion at intervals from February to June in the open air. . . . An excellent little Onion for spring sowing is the blanc très hâtif de la Reine (Early White Queen). When sown in March it is ready in May, but as it is little more than an inch when fully developed, it is grown more in private than in market gardens."

(Weathers, *French Market-Gardening*, 1909, 185, 187, 188)

* *See author's note on page 91*

88

ONIONS

There are many types of garden onions and many different ways to make sure you have garden onions for your family every day of the year.

Short-day onions: These require eleven to twelve hours of sunlight each day to form a globe, which makes them best suited for growing in the southern United States As a general rule, think of drawing a line between San Francisco and Washington, D.C. If you live near the line, intermediate-day onions are probably best for you. North of the line, you would grow long-day onions. South of the line you would grow short-day onions. Short-day onions generally do not store well.

Intermediate-day onions: These need twelve to fourteen hours of sunlight each day to form a globe. Intermediate onions do not store as well as long-day onions, but they store better than short-day onions.

Long-day onions: These are best suited for growing in the northern United States. This is because long-day onions need a minimum of fourteen hours of daylight in a day before they will begin to form bulbs. Long-day onions such as Yellow Spanish globe store well for months after they are picked and "cured" by letting them dry in sunlight for a day or two. These are generally the onions sold in grocery stores. In the northern United States, these onions are grown in summer and then stored for eating over winter. These onions can also be stored, without being picked, where they grew in the garden if they are covered with a foot of straw, leaves, hay, or grass clippings to keep them from freezing. At our house, we leave some

long-day onions unprotected in the open garden all winter for fresh picking. Some of the smallest and largest bulbs will die when the ground freezes, but I have found that the medium-sized bulbs can sometimes withstand being in the open garden all winter and can be picked in January and February for fresh eating. They may have some damage from freezing, but if they are used fairly quickly in the kitchen—within several hours of being picked—the quality of the onion will be fine, in my experience.

Topset onions: These are perennial onions which form small bulbs at the top of the plant, as the name suggests. In the northern United States, these onions are valuable because they mature in April and May, far sooner than globe onions. In early spring, the shoots of topset onions can be eaten as green onions. Also called Egyptian Walking onions and sometimes tree onions.

Multiplier onions: These onions get their name because you plant a small bulb and over the gardening season that bulb will multiply to become four to fifteen new small bulbs. Multiplier onions can sometimes be quite large and have been known to store for several years without rotting. Also called potato onions.

Bunching onions: Bunching onions can be planted in January and February in a cold frame or hotbed. Also called green onions (of potato salad fame).

Caleb Warnock

Common chives: These perennial herbs appear quickly in spring and then almost just as quickly form flowers. Common chives slowly dry over the summer. Then in fall, the plant regenerates and flowers a second time. Chive flowers are edible and are prized for their sweet onion flavor. They can be divided by the roots to create new plants or can be grown from the seed found in the topset bulbs. To get fresh chives far into winter and earlier in spring, transplant a clump from your main garden into a cold frame or hotbed for winter use. Garlic chives, also called oriental chives, flower only once a year. Their garlic flavor is popular in Asian cooking. I grow both in my perennial herb garden.

WHEN TO PLANT

Long-day onions such as Yellow Spanish globe can be planted from seed in a cold frame or hotbed anytime beginning in January. Depending on the weather, they may be slow to germinate, so be patient. Do not let them overheat—they are sensitive to hot temperatures on sunny days in February and March in a hotbed, and I have scalded some to death. I recommend planting these alone in a hotbed (instead of sharing a hotbed with other winter vegetables) and propping open the lid on sunny days. Starting your own onions from seed this way will save you money, compared to buying onion starts for planting in April.

91

* Author's note: "Blanc Hâtif de Paris" is no longer available in the United States though it was sold here until the 1970s. I was close to finding some seed for this variety in the US federal germplasm seed bank, where it had been collected from France. For whatever reason, that seed was not available, so the federal government found some for me in a seed bank in the Netherlands, which I planted in February in a hotbed in my backyard garden with television cameras rolling (I invited the media, to bring attention to the plight of nearly extinct vegetable seed). Onion seed is only considered viable for one to two years, and the seed that was flown in in 2012 was marked 2005—a common problem with seed banks, which do not have enough staff and resources to regularly grow aging seed. Because it was so old, I planted the seed as soon as I got it. It took a staggering 39 days for the first seed to germinate—far longer than is normal. I am happy to say that as of July 2012, I have several dozen of these onions growing happily in my garden. I hope to make the seed available as soon as possible to other winter gardeners who would like to help revive this nearly extinct, but important, winter variety. When seed is available, I will list it on calebwarnock.blogspot.com.

Onions

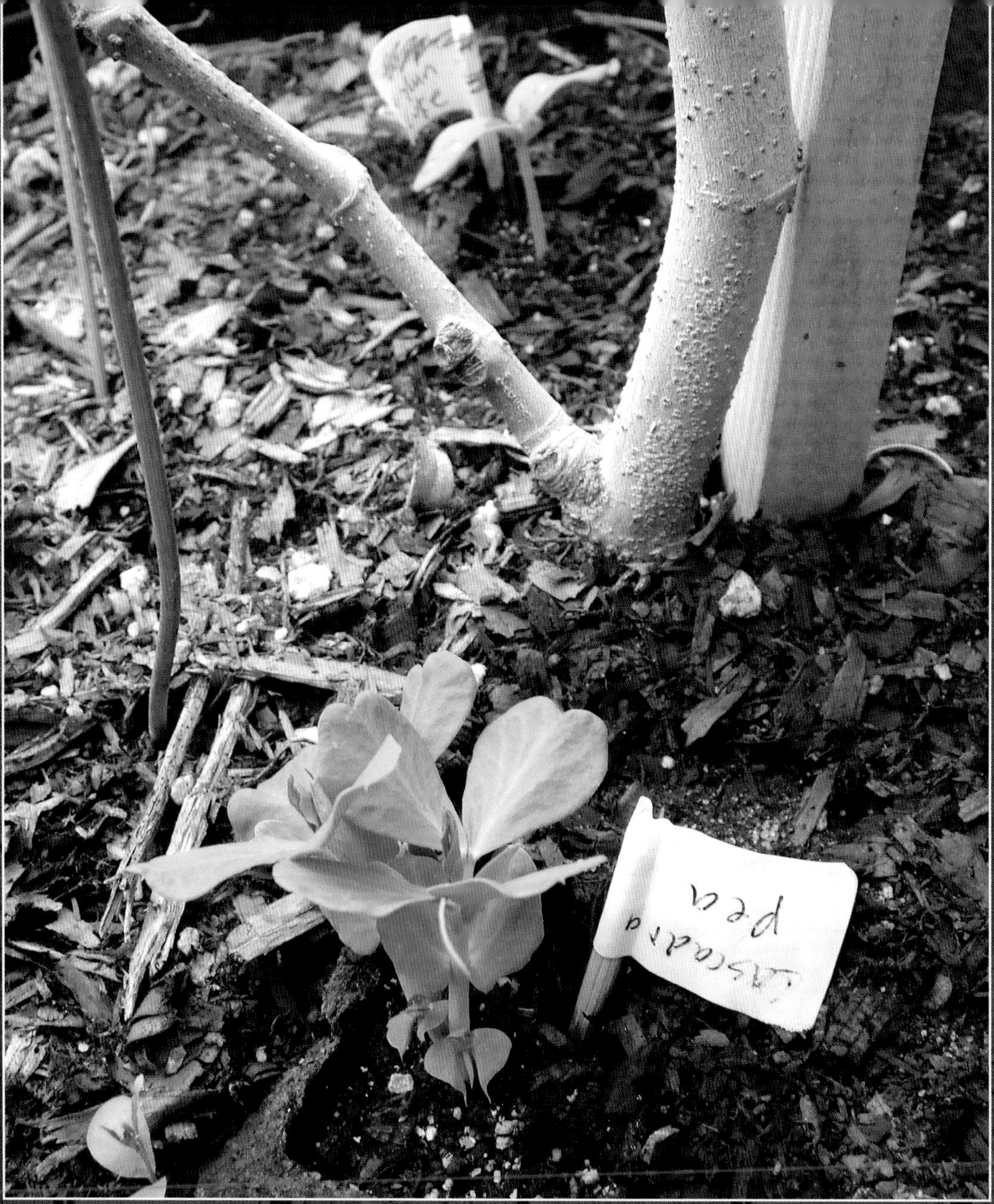
Cascadia
pea

PEAS

RECOMMENDED VARIETIES FOR THE WINTER GARDEN

Tom Thumb is a variety of pea that can withstand repeated hard frosts, and it also sprouts amazingly well in winter when planted in a hotbed and grows faster than lettuce in bitter temperatures. This variety of pea can be planted any month of the year, but in a winter hotbed it does like some air circulation—take the lid off on sunny days. But don't forget to close the lid at nighttime.

The Lincoln variety resists hard frosts when mature and will stand a long time if covered with a cold frame.

Cascadia is the earliest commonly available pea I know of, which makes it a natural choice for autumn planting and use in hotbeds.

More work needs to be done by winter gardeners to test different varieties of peas for winter use. Next winter I will be testing a variety of peas both in and out of cold frames, and I will post my results on my blog. If you would like to trial winter peas, or any winter vegetable, you can share your results with me by e-mailing me at caleb-warnock@yahoo.com.

WHEN TO PLANT

To give peas time to actually produce a crop, you will need to plant in the first week of August, generally. These August peas should be planted directly in the garden soil.

After your early August planting, you can plant peas every month throughout winter if you use a hotbed. But keep in mind that these peas will grow more slowly with each passing day as the daylight wanes. Because of this, it is likely that your early August crop and possibly your September crop will be the only peas ready to eat before early spring. For example, Tom Thumb peas planted in November will only be three inches tall in January, but they will slowly begin to grow faster after the winter solstice, which is generally in the last week of December. Winter solstice marks the shortest day and longest night of the year, and each day after gradually brings more sunlight. (The vernal equinox in late March marks the time when day and night are equal—and after the equinox is when plants and gardens begin to shake off winter.)

HOW TO GROW

Luckily, peas are particularly well-suited to winter cultivation because they are self-pollinating. This means that the male part of the pea flower pollinates the female part of the flower before the flower even opens, so there is no need for bees or moths or other insect pollinators. So you can grow peas in cold frames in the dead of winter and still get a harvest. When the peas are ready, pick and eat!

POTATOES

My wife, Charmayne, is fond of saying that every family should have a working knowledge of how to grow potatoes. Potatoes are a must-have for winter eating. There are some tricks to making your potato harvest easier, especially if you have what I call "porcelain soil"—soil that is hard and dense and so full of clay that it is better suited for making plates than growing potatoes.

RECOMMENDED VARIETIES FOR THE WINTER GARDEN

Any variety of spud can be used for winter gardening. I regularly grow Red Pontiac, Yukon Gold, and russet. To be clear, you do not grow potatoes in winter—you simply leave them in the garden where you grew them, as described in this chapter, so you can eat them fresh all winter.

And don't be afraid to experiment with new varieties of potatoes. In the upcoming year, I'm looking forward to trying a potato that is red inside and out, called Mountain Rose, from Seed Savers Exchange. They also have some other great potato varieties that are hard to find elsewhere.

THREE METHODS FOR WINTER POTATOES

1 Compost Potatoes

Plant your potatoes in spring as usual. But instead of planting potatoes in your native soil, dig a trench or use a raised garden bed. Put in your seed potatoes and sprinkle in some blood meal and bonemeal (this is organic fertilizer you can get anywhere) and cover with at least ten inches of compost—no soil. Don't be surprised if the potatoes take a month or more before sprouting above the compost. Water them with the rest of the garden.

When winter arrives, you can leave the potatoes exactly where you grew them if you place bags of yard leaves over the soil to keep it from freezing. Then simply dig up the potatoes as needed throughout winter.

2 Straw Potatoes (also called the French Method)

Another easy way to grow potatoes in terrible soil is to dig a trench or use a raised bed filled with straw instead of soil. Follow the same directions from the first method, beginning with planting your potatoes in early spring as usual, except use straw instead of compost. When winter comes, cover with additional straw or with bags of leaves to make sure the potatoes don't freeze. You can then harvest them throughout winter as needed. Both this method and the compost method tend to keep potatoes sweeter and less starchy through winter.

3 Cellaring Without a Root Cellar

Whether you grow your potatoes in compost, straw, or in your garden soil, you can store them for winter in an unheated, dark garage. Or if your garage has windows, in a box that will keep the potatoes in darkness.

This method doesn't require going outside in winter to dig potatoes, but the potatoes stored this way will taste a little more like grocery store potatoes—more starchy than sweet, but definitely still great to eat. It is critical that potatoes and any other vegetables you might store in the garage never come into contact with concrete. Make sure you have wood or several layers of cardboard between your potatoes and a concrete floor. Concrete is a strong desiccant, meaning it will immediately begin to wick moisture out of your vegetables, and they will begin to rot within a week or so. And never wash potatoes before storing them in your garage. You should store them with the dirt on them, exactly the way you dug them out of the garden—not with clumps of dirt, but with the dirt residue they come out of the ground or compost bed with. Unwashed potatoes store far better, and far longer, than potatoes that are washed. Of course you will wash them when it comes time to cook them.

Caleb Warnock

TWO NOTES ABOUT POTATOES

1 Remember—don't eat the small potatoes! Save your small ones for planting in next year's crop. Because potatoes are genetic clones and are not planted by seed, you don't have to worry about small potatoes growing only small potatoes. The small potatoes from your garden will yield another excellent crop of large potatoes each year, and you won't have to buy seed potatoes again for at least several years, which can save you a lot of money. (An old-time gardener at one of my speeches recently argued with me on this point. He said you need to use the large potatoes for seed potatoes or your potatoes will be small. I have not had this problem, but if you are worried about it, use your large potatoes for seed.)

I have read that eventually home-grown potatoes can begin to become disease-prone and therefore need to be replaced with commercially produced seed potatoes (which go through a rigorous growing process to avoid disease) every few years. This is probably a good idea.

2 You should never use grocery store potatoes as seed potatoes. Store potatoes have usually been sprayed with a chemical to retard sprouting—that is why they don't immediately sprout shoots in the light and warmth of the store. Because of that chemical, they are more likely to rot in your garden than to grow another potato. So grow your own organic potatoes at home; you don't have to worry about eating chemicals, and you can save some of your own crop to plant for the next year, just as families have done for thousands of years.

Knowledge from Historic Gardens and Gardeners
•RUTABAGAS•

"[Rutabagas] suffer from very hot weather, but are not affected by frost, one of their chief merits being their extreme hardiness. They are best sown, where the crop is to be grown, in May and June. . . .

". . . They are in the best condition for table use if lifted before they have reached their full growth. The Swedish or Turnip-rooted Cabbage [other names for rutabagas] is an excellent vegetable deserving to be more used than it is."

(Vilmorin-Andrieux, *The Vegetable Garden*, 166–167)

RUTABAGAS

What can I say? I love rutabaga, probably because it has forever changed our holiday eating. A few years ago on a bitter February evening, my wife and I were at Thorrablót, the midwinter Icelandic Viking feast hosted each year in Spanish Fork, Utah, by the Icelandic Association of Utah. This traditional feast is attended by hundreds of people and is famous for serving authentic Icelandic fare. My wife and I have no Icelandic ancestry, but we have been to Thorrablót a half dozen times. On this particular occasion, however, I was served something I had never seen before—it looked like mashed potatoes, but it was orange. And the flavor was something I had never experienced before—superb and new. And if you like to eat like I do, it's not often that you find something truly new to fall in love with.

I ate the dish and had seconds, and I started asking around, trying to figure out what this was. I was eventually pointed to the kitchen, where the busy chef was a bit perplexed about my interest. He explained to me that this was traditional Icelandic mashed potatoes, an old tradition. The ingredients? Simple, he said. Equal parts potatoes, carrots, and rutabagas, boiled together and then mashed with some butter, salt, and pepper.

I was captivated. This dish has now become a favorite part of our Thanksgiving and Christmas feasts, with potatoes, carrots, and rutabagas grown in our own garden, of course. The taste is fantastic. Try it for yourself.

RECOMMENDED VARIETIES FOR THE WINTER GARDEN

Call me a garden geek, but rutabagas also excite me because they are one of the few open-pollinated vegetables that have been improved in recent history.

For hundreds of years, improving vegetables was a wide practice (the orange carrot is a good example of a relatively recent vegetable "invention," as I explain in my first book). Swiss botanist Gaspard Bauhin is credited with discovering rutabaga growing wild in Sweden in 1620, and from then until now little work has been done on breeding improved varieties. But Frank Morton of Shoulder to Shoulder Farm in Philomath, Oregon, has begun working to change that. He is one of few people in the United States who work to improve heirloom (open-pollinated) vegetables. Most new seeds are hybrid, meaning the seed is artificially pollinated and the parentage is kept secret so that no one else can produce the seed who is not the "owner." But open-pollinated seeds can be grown and sold by anyone, so there is not a lot of money in creating new varieties. Nevertheless, all the vegetables we eat today—both hybrid and open-pollinated—exist because someone in history worked to improve them and then let the world have the seed. That is part of our food heritage, and Frank Morton is continuing that tradition. He is an owner of the Wild Garden Seed company, and he introduced Joan rutabaga to the world in 2011. I was one of the early growers of this seed, which exploded in popularity in 2012 seed catalogs.

Wild Garden Seed, when introducing Joan rutabaga to the world, wrote, "After sitting on this secret for several years, we now feel free to tell all; this is the best all round rutabaga you can buy for flavor (sweetest and best texture), uniformity (round, yellow fleshed, purple topped), and good resistance to club root."[1] And the description is true—this new heirloom has a wonderful flavor. Joan is the rutabaga variety I prefer now.

WHEN TO PLANT & HOW TO GROW

Rutabaga performs best in the garden if planted in early fall instead of in the spring. And the flavor of rutabaga is improved by frost, so win-win. The Joan rutabaga I plant during the last week of July is ready to harvest for Thanksgiving dinner and is grown in the open garden without any protection. To get a faster crop, plant in mid-July and cover with a cold frame beginning in late September or early October, depending on the weather. Rutabaga is an extremely hardy vegetable, but it will begin to die after the ground has been frozen solid for a week or two.

Notes

1. Wild Garden Seed, "Joan."

The Misunderstood Rutabaga

The purple-top globe turnip and the rutabaga look startlingly alike, and this causes a lot of confusion. But famed writer Garrison Keillor wants America to pay closer attention.

"They're not alike at all," he once said on his radio show, *A Prairie Home Companion*. "Rutabagas have a pleasant yellow-orange color, large friendly-looking leaves, and a smooth dense texture. Turnips are fish-belly white and purple on top like a bad bruise and have hairy leaves and taste brackish, like swampwater. Rutabagas are the root crop that any sensible person would prefer" (Keillor, "RCA script").

Knowledge from Historic Gardens and Gardeners
•SPINACH•

"At one time French gardeners used to grow Spinach on hot-beds, on which young plants were pricked out about 4 in. apart in November, so as to be ready for gathering from December to March. . . .

". . . About the middle of February Spinach may be sown at intervals of two or three weeks, until the end of July."

(Weathers, *French Market-Gardening*, 1909, 199, 200)

SPINACH

RECOMMENDED VARIETY FOR THE WINTER GARDEN

America spinach is an extremely hardy winter spinach that can stand outside all winter without any protection at all. This is a Bloomsdale-type with a great taste.

OTHER WINTER SPINACH VARIETIES

Bloomsdale Long Standing: A small-leafed spinach that overwinters to produce well in spring.

Bloomsdale Winter: A good fall and winter spinach with dark green leaves.

Cold Resistant Savoy: Resistant to both cold and heat, as well as slow to go to seed, a trait which provides a longer window for harvest.

Guntmadingen Winter: A rare Swiss heirloom variety, which is exceptionally winter hardy.

Haldenstein: Another Swiss variety named after a Swiss village, which has been keeping this seed line alive since before the First World War. A great fall crop; winter spinach with large leaves.

Verdil: A giant-type spinach, which is an excellent producer in winter, even under a foot of snow.

WHEN TO PLANT & HOW TO GROW

In my garden, America spinach is slow to grow, so it's important to start this spinach in early August or even late July—this will give it time to grow large enough for a bigger winter harvest. You can expect to begin harvesting baby leaves in January. Harvest the outer leaves, leaving the leaves in the center to continue to grow out. Harvested this way, winter spinach will continue to produce fresh spinach into summer.

Knowledge from Historic Gardens and Gardeners
•SQUASH•

Author's note: *"Marrow" is another term for squash.*

"[Marrows] are an important crop when the fruits can be secured early in the season. The Bush Marrows, as well as the creeping kinds, might be very easily established early in the year in the following way: About February, or early in March, dig out a few spadefuls of soil where each plant is to grow. The hole thus made should be filled with a layer about a foot thick of hot manure, and covered with about 6 in. of nice, rich, gritty mould. When the rank heat, if any, has subsided and the temperature is about 70° to 75° Fahr., two or three Marrow seeds should be sown about 2 in. deep in the centre of each little bed, and after being watered in, should be covered with a cloche. As many little hot-beds as are required can be made in this way, allowing enough space between each for the development of the plants later on. After germination air is given as freely as possible, considering the weather, and by the middle or end of May, or before that period in many parts, it will be possible to remove the cloches altogether. Attention to copious waterings and pinching the shoots afterwards constitute the chief cultural details to secure an abundance of early Marrows."

(Weathers, *French Market-Gardening*, 1909, 62–63)

SQUASH

I am just beginning my experiments with squash in the winter garden, outside the geothermal greenhouse. In the greenhouse, I've had great success growing early zucchini. For more information about that, look in the geothermal greenhouse chapter. The reason that I haven't done more with squash in winter already is because it is not necessary—I put winter squash in my cellar and garage, where it lasts all winter, through April. This includes pumpkins, winter squashes, and rampicante zucchini. So I haven't needed winter squash because I already have it.

Nevertheless, you can give your squash an early start by using a hotbed. Timing is critical here—remember, your squash plants are going to have to stay inside some kind of cover until after the last frost. And squash plants grow fast. So my advice is to wait until April, unless you are just dying to have zucchini, which you could start in a hotbed in mid to late March if it had three feet of manure under it, like tomatoes and cantaloupes. Even in April, I'd still use three feet of manure to heat the bed because squash are notoriously tender plants—almost as bad as basil. And once a squash begins to grow in a hotbed, it will need a higher cover and a large enough space to spread out—and remember once again that you are not going to be able to take the cover off until after the last frost, which is in mid-May where I live.

Knowledge from Historic Gardens and Gardeners
•STRAWBERRIES•

"Amongst important fruits, Strawberries may be looked upon as being particularly suited for growing under lights or cloches to produce early crops. At present these are grown in pots in greenhouses, close to the glass, and require considerable time and attention in regard to watering, syringing, regulation of temperature, and keeping free from mildew. Grown under cloches, or in beds that will accommodate the frames and lights used for salads, it would be possible to secure early crops of Strawberries in spring from young plantations without going to the trouble of lifting the plants and potting them in the autumn. For instance, in the case of beds, it would be possible after placing the frames and lights over the plants, to fill in the pathways with manure from which heat would be generated in the frames in accordance with the requirements of the season. A certain amount of the short, warm manure could also be worked in between the rows of plants without disturbing the roots, and when the fruits were swelling, a layer of clean litter could be added for the sake of cleanliness. In this way the Strawberries would come into bearing more quickly, and watering and ventilation could be attended to without inconvenience. Once the fruits are gathered, the frames and lights, and manure in the pathways, may be used for other purposes. Of course Strawberries grown in pots could also be forced in the frames if necessary."

(Weathers, *French Market-Gardening*, 1909, 60–61)

STRAWBERRIES

One of the hardest parts about watching autumn transition into winter is having to say good-bye to fall strawberries. It seems that every year, as the first hard freezes arrive, the strawberries somehow sense their own doom and flush with ripe berries. Cold frames can be used to extend the season for any strawberry plants you have, regardless of variety. Simply place a frame over the strawberry plants where they sit.

Strawberries are a perennial plant, and they are one of the first plants to put out leaves in the spring. If you have extra space in a hotbed, or if you just really want to experiment, you can keep strawberry plants leafy green all winter. But the plants won't begin to flower and produce fruit until March. They will be a few weeks ahead of your other strawberry plants, but consider that these plants take up a lot of space and don't produce anything edible all winter. So if you are going to trial winter strawberries, like I have, you'll be sacrificing some space that could be going toward a vegetable that will produce fresh food all winter, like lettuce, kale, chard, or Chinese cabbage, for example.

SWISS CHARD

Swiss chard is one of the best parts of the winter garden. Although this delicious leafy green can be grown in myriad colors in summer—yellow, red, purple, green— once the ground freezes, all the plants tend to turn to one of two colors: deep green or dark purple.

The torn leaves of winter chard are a great addition to a salad. One of my favorite uses is to mince the leaves and add them to omelets. For a different taste, sauté the leaves in butter and spritz with lime juice or balsamic vinegar. In Italy (and at my house) the stems of winter chard are chopped and added to pasta.

RECOMMENDED VARIETIES FOR THE WINTER GARDEN

Any variety of chard can be used for winter growing.

PLANTING, GROWING, HARVESTING

Sow seed for Swiss chard as usual in the late spring or early summer. Mature chard is quite winter hardy and will not need to be covered with a cold frame until early winter—sometime in November usually. In winter, the larger outer leaves, which are the oldest leaves, will slowly die back, but don't be tempted to clean them up. Leave them as they are because they act as sort of a blanket for the taproot and growth crown of the plant. Chard will grow new leaves from the center of the plant all winter if kept in a cold frame, and it is these young, tender leaves that you will harvest and eat. Simply cut the leaves off as you want them.

In spring, when the weather has warmed to the point where the cold frame protecting the chard can be removed, the plants will begin to bolt and go to seed, ending their life cycle.

Knowledge from Historic Gardens and Gardeners
· TOMATOES ·

"In most parts of the kingdom it is dangerous to place Tomato plants in the open air till the end of May or early in June, owing to the frosts and cold nights. If, however, hot-beds of the regulation width . . . were prepared, and a gentle heat from the manure were secured, it would be quite possible to sow Tomato seeds under a cloche or two as early as January or February, in the gritty mould that would be placed over the manure. The strongest plants would be pricked out in due course."

(Weathers, *French Market-Gardening*, 1909, 61)

TOMATOES

Having fresh tomatoes from your garden twelve months of the year is possible if you use a geothermal greenhouse. Mature tomato plants will continue to produce new tomatoes all winter long. For more information about tomatoes in the geothermal greenhouse, please refer to that chapter.

Without a geothermal greenhouse, tomatoes can be given a head start of several months by using a hotbed—if you are careful and if you use the right varieties.

RECOMMENDED VARIETIES FOR THE WINTER GARDEN

Several varieties of ultra-early, open-pollinated tomatoes include Vee One, Mountain Princess, Silvery Fir Tree, and Snow Fairy. Out of all of these, Snow Fairy is by far the most tolerant of the bitter cold in my winter garden tests, but it too eventually succumbs to near-zero temperatures in January and February in a hotbed unless it is given the same kind of special treatment as cantaloupes. This means you will need a hotbed with three feet of manure underneath it if you want to plant Snow Fairy tomatoes in January or February—and even then a night below zero could kill the tomato.

WHEN TO PLANT & HOW TO GROW

My recommendation for beginners who are looking for results and aren't just experimenting is to wait until early March. Build a three-foot-deep, manure-heated hotbed and wait a week before planting anything in it to make sure the heat has begun to come up from below. Start your tomato plants in the house, where they will have warmer

temperatures at night. But watch them carefully and transplant them to the hotbed immediately upon the first sign of sprouting—even before the first leaves have unfolded. The faster they are taken out to the hotbed, the better their chances of survival. Their growth will immediately slow down once they are put in the hotbed, but the strongest plants will slowly and surely begin to take hold. Keep them covered with a low cover as long as possible and then, when they get too tall, add another layer of wood under the lid to raise it up. Take caution: As I said in the cantaloupe chapter, many winter garden vegetables love to have the cover removed on a sunny, warm winter day when temperatures are in the forties or fifties. And many don't need any cover at all, day or night, beginning in mid-April. But tomatoes do not fall in this group. My recommendation for tomatoes is that you remove the cover only for a moment at a time to check on them and only on the warmest, sunniest days. And never, ever keep them uncovered until you are sure all danger of frost has passed—imagine working to nurture a hotbed tomato, only to have it freeze in a rogue May frost.

TURNIPS

RECOMMENDED VARIETIES FOR THE WINTER GARDEN

Any variety of turnip can be used for winter growing, but there are two varieties that I prefer to grow any time of year—Boule d'Or and the common purple-top globe.

Boule d'Or, or "golden ball," is a 150-year-old French variety with unique, pale yellow flesh and a mild, fine flavor that bears almost no resemblance to the traditional turnip flavor. Although this is a great turnip for soups and roasted vegetables, it does have a couple of drawbacks: It will not store in a root cellar or garage like the common turnip will. And like all turnips, the longer it stays in the garden and the larger it gets, the more its flavor shifts until it has a hot and sour flavor. Because most of us are probably not going to be making a lot of soup or roasted vegetables in summer, and because this turnip will not tolerate storage, it is best grown for fall and winter harvest instead of being planted in the spring.

The common purple-top globe is the traditional turnip most of us are familiar with. This turnip stores for months when boxed (more on that in a moment).

WHEN TO PLANT

Like winter beets, winter turnips get woody and tough as they age, and the larger the turnip, the less likely it is to make it through winter. The best-tasting winter turnips are young, which means that you will need to plant your seed in early August. If you plant when it is too hot—late July, for example—the seed will not germinate as well. But the young turnips need enough time to form a good root before the daylight shortens.

•TURNIPS•

"Turnips are now grown as a forced or 'primeur' crop on hot-beds more than formerly. Early in January a bed is made up to give a temperature about 70° to 80° Fahr. . . .

". . . In about seven or eight weeks after sowing the seeds . . . the young Turnips are fit to pull. . . .

". . . The variety of Turnip favoured by the Parisian grower is called 'Marteau' or 'Half-long Vertu,' owing to its quick growth and excellent quality. It is the variety *par excellence* for the first early crops."

(Weathers, *French Market-Gardening*, 1909, 201, 202, 203)

114

Author's note: *I have only been able to find Marteau seed at gourmetseed.com. Marteau is a long, cylindrical white turnip, which grew slowly in my winter hotbed but was ready to eat in late May. But it had been crowded under lettuces in my hotbed and would have done better and grown faster without being shaded by lettuce leaves.*

HOW TO GROW & HARVEST

Turnips grow slowly and then form a globe quickly, just like beets. Cover your turnips with a cold frame in late fall, before the ground begins to freeze. I grow my winter turnips in the same cold frame as my Swiss chard, and throughout the winter, the turnip will grow shiny new leaves—almost waxy but tender—which can be picked just like chard to be added to salads. Harvest the turnip globes as needed. If the temperature dips below freezing both night and day for several days in a row, the turnip root may suffer some frost damage, but I have found that if picked and used immediately for cooking, the flavor and quality is not affected.

BOXING TURNIPS

Turnips, except for Boule d'Or, can be boxed for winter use just like beets. This means picking your turnips in early winter or late fall and storing them in a garage or root cellar for later use. The good news is that if you box your turnips, you won't have to go out into the winter weather in your backyard to harvest them.

To box turnips, use a plastic storage box or line a cardboard box with a plastic garbage bag. Fill with wet pine shavings (you can get them inexpensively at pet stores or farm supply stores). Take the mature turnips from your late fall garden and trim the leafy greens an inch above the top of the root, but don't cut the top of the root. Put the mature turnips in the box in layers, and cover the turnips completely. Store the box in your unheated garage or root cellar in darkness through the winter, taking the turnips out as you want them.

TENDER WINTER TURNIP GREENS

When boxed for winter and stored in the cellar or garage, turnips will grow leaves in the dark. These tender leaves make for great eating, either fresh or sautéed. And they will grow back each time you cut them! Make sure you don't cover the box with anything, so the leaves will have room to grow. Turnip leaves grown like this will be pale with hints of green.

THE GEOTHERMAL WINTER GREENHOUSE

A winter greenhouse is not necessary to feed your family twelve months a year—let me be clear about that up front. A geothermal greenhouse can be expensive and difficult to build. So why talk about something that is expensive, hard, and not necessary? Well . . .

Here are ten reasons why I have a geothermal greenhouse:

1 A Geothermal Greenhouse Is the Most Useful Greenhouse

A geothermal greenhouse has zero ongoing costs because it never uses any electricity or artificial heat. Traditional greenhouses must either be artificially heated in winter at great expense or they cannot be used in winter at all because they freeze at night. But a geothermal greenhouse never freezes. And a geothermal greenhouse can be used to grow vegetables every single day of the year. So if you are going to invest in a greenhouse, you might as well spend your money on the most useful, and most self-sufficient, greenhouse in existence.

Warm Winter Gardening

Imagine this: It's been below freezing for days. There is a bitter, raging winter wind and snow and ice are outside. It's true—the hotbeds and cold frames in the backyard garden will be fine and will continue to produce food for your family. But there's nothing like being inside the geothermal greenhouse while winter rages outside—this is a winter garden you can relax in! It's warm, it's sunny, there is never any wind, and you are surrounded by green plants. I find myself taking much, much longer to pick a winter salad than is necessary. I can do real gardening, in the middle of winter, without a coat!

3 Seed Starting

Before I had a winter greenhouse, I started seeds in the house. And because I have a huge garden—and because I'm not happy if I'm away from the garden for too long—I would plant hundreds of seeds, even thousands. I took over all the kitchen counters and the dining room buffet. I bought complicated indoor lighting systems and electric heat mats and mini-greenhouse kits. But nothing starts seeds as well as my geothermal greenhouse. And I can stuff the greenhouse full of plants and no one cares. I don't have to worry about trying to keep lights a half inch above my baby plants (which is impossible, and the plants in the house often ended up leggy and weak). And before my greenhouse, there was never enough room or space to start all the seeds I wanted, so I always ended up buying some starts every year. No more.

4 Year-Round Tomatoes

Geothermal greenhouses can grow fresh tomatoes all winter long. And I can start tomato plants from seed in November, December, January, or February. As I write this in February, six varieties of tomatoes are growing in my geothermal greenhouse, and I just picked my fresh tomatoes today to bring in the house. People love to get my fresh winter tomatoes as gifts—sometimes people beg for them. Having fresh, backyard tomatoes that taste far better than anything you can buy in the grocery store makes my wife love me more than she already did. Tomatoes are one of the best reasons to have a winter greenhouse.

5 Gardeners Dream of Greenhouses

If you are a green-blooded gardener like me, you dream of having a greenhouse. Greenhouses have been an obsession of gardeners for centuries because they allow you to do things you simply cannot do any other way. But no other greenhouse even comes close to being as useful every day of the year as a geothermal greenhouse. Not even close!

6 Off-the-Grid Self-Sufficiency

There is no electricity to my greenhouse. No solar kit, no batteries, no propane heat, no artificial heat of any kind, period. No technology that can break down. My greenhouse is heated entirely by the sun during the day and the heat of the earth at night. It is built to outlast me. No matter what happens (knock on wood), I should be able to feed my family out of the greenhouse every winter.

7 Disaster Preparedness

This January, something happened that every homeowner dreads: our furnace broke down. We had already installed natural gas wall heaters on both floors of the house, so we didn't miss a beat (or spend a single cold minute) while we waited several days for the professionals to fix the problem. But that little experience just goes to show that the heat we take for granted in winter is not infallible. What if there was an earthquake or major disaster and the house was destroyed or unsafe to live in? If there was a major earthquake along the Wasatch Front in Utah, the likelihood is that the threat of aftershocks would make it unsafe for us to stay in the house, perhaps for weeks—even if the earthquake did not shut off the gas and electricity. My greenhouse is constructed of eight-inch by eight-inch timbers below ground, and framing two-by-fours above ground, which means it is highly likely that it will withstand a major earthquake unscathed. And because it will not freeze, our family could stay in the greenhouse in the event of a terrible disaster—it would not be the most comfortable stay, but we wouldn't freeze to death, and we would have fresh food. These are things that I hope never, ever happen. But it does make me sleep a little better at night.

8 Kids Play Outside in Winter

One of the advantages of my geothermal greenhouse that I did not foresee was its value for keeping the kids happy during winter. They love to play in the greenhouse! Xander, who is six, and Ada, who is two, were both out there with me today, in early February, and they didn't want to leave. The greenhouse is warm, and they can dig, play, and look at the plants and flowers, and they don't have to wear a coat or gloves. Plus, there are always a lot of interesting, fun things to do in a greenhouse—plant seeds, water the plants, pick the tomatoes, cut the lettuce, watch the ladybugs. Xander spends hours in the greenhouse in winter digging tunnels and holes, making bridges, and making up games and stories in his head. So much better than putting him in front of the television!

9 Exotic Plants

My proudest single gardening moment ever may be sprouting not one but two banana trees from seed, in January, in Utah, in my geothermal greenhouse. At this moment (February 9, 2012), in my greenhouse, I have an orange tree, a fig tree, a pineapple plant, Inca berry, acai berry, stevia, and those two banana trees growing in my greenhouse—not to mention not one, not two, but four cantaloupe plants! It's simply fun. And these are all things I never could have grown without a geothermal greenhouse. None of these plants are necessary for my family's welfare, but they make me smile.

The Geothermal Winter Greenhouse

10 Free Therapy

Winter is especially hard on gardeners. When people ask me about my greenhouse, I often tell them the first reason I had it built was because the greenhouse was cheaper than therapy. There is nothing in the world like standing in my greenhouse during a winter snowstorm, listening to the snowflakes ping as they hit the roof. I can pick vegetables at my leisure as the wind howls. Or I can merely sit and think and enjoy the silence. Or I can take the little kids out with me and let them play and work with me. Or water the plants, or plant seeds, or prune, or plan, or re-arrange. Watch the ladybugs. Watch the chickens, horse, and cows out the window. I check the progress of both my seedlings and my mature plants each day, and I often find myself wishing I had more time to waste in my greenhouse. When life begins to feel too crazy, I go outside, feed the chickens, and then visit the greenhouse. And I can breathe again. (I can probably literally breathe better. There are a lot of green plants in a small space, producing lots of oxygen!)

THE WALIPINI

I had to invent the plans for my greenhouse from whole cloth because I had never seen another one like it. My concept was that if my root cellar does not freeze all winter because of the heat of the earth, I needed a way to put a clear "roof" on a cellar and keep in enough heat to turn the cellar into a greenhouse. I became more interested while attending a greenhouse design class taught by the local master gardeners. The teacher showed a slide of a pit greenhouse in Utah, built into a hole in the ground with a polycarbonate, A-frame roof. I knew instantly that that was what I was trying to design on my own. The teacher said he had been in the greenhouse once and that it seemed to work.

From that point on, I could think of almost nothing else. I spent probably a hundred hours researching pit greenhouses, only to find that little information was available. I was particularly interested in the ancient pit greenhouse concept practiced by the Aymara Indians of Bolivia, apparently beginning even a thousand years ago. This was documented by the Benson Institute at Brigham Young University in a research bulletin. Researchers had theoretically designed a modern version "specifically for the area of La Paz, Bolivia." The ancient idea is called a "Walipini" in the Aymara Indian language, which means "place of warmth." According to the Benson Institute research, "the Walipini utilizes nature's resources to provide a warm, stable, well-lit environment for year-round vegetable production."[1]

This research was exactly what I was looking for. The problem was that I could find no evidence that anyone had ever actually built the Walipini described in the Benson Institute documents (they have since built one). The bulletin itself talks about what researchers will do *when* they build it. But I couldn't find anyone who had ever seen one in person or operated one.

Eventually, based on all of my research—which went far beyond the Walipini—I decided that there was no expert to consult and that I would simply have to build a pit greenhouse to the best of my own design ability, based on what I had read. Several sources suggested that installing large pipes into the earth would help create a current of above-freezing air, which would circulate in the greenhouse at night, when any unheated greenhouse is most vulnerable to freezing temperatures.

I don't have any talent for straight lines or construction, but I knew a trustworthy builder who I hoped would be willing to work with me on the concept. I designed a primitive sketch of what I wanted and called the builder. It took a bit of talking to explain what I was trying to accomplish. Of course the builder had never heard of such a thing, and he was a little concerned that I didn't actually know anyone who owned anything similar or who had ever used such a thing effectively. He suggested I use a Google program I had never heard of before called SketchUp—a free, three-dimensional architectural design program developed on the Internet by Google, bless them. I learned how to use the program and made my design. My builder used the design to make his own, refined version with real measurements, and we were ready to begin construction. (I have made my original design available to the public, free of charge. To view it, search for "Caleb Warnock greenhouse" in Google SketchUp).

The builder's first concern was that the walls of the pit could eventually collapse under the weight of the earth. He said it was too dangerous to build without something called "dead men"—huge wooden ties that attach to the interior wooden walls, sticking out several feet into the surrounding earth. These ties essentially keep the retaining walls anchored firmly into the surrounding earth, so that the walls don't one day collapse. The builder would only agree to build the structure if it were designed with these "dead men" anchors—so called, he told me, because without them, the people who go inside the structure are likely to one day be killed in a collapse. That alone made me hugely grateful I'd hired an expert.

My greenhouse is twelve feet by nine feet. I didn't want to build it too large, because I knew from my research that the larger the interior space, the more vulnerable it might be to freezing at night without artificial heat. The pit was dug eight feet deep. At the bottom of the eight-foot hole, I asked the builder to put in two large pipes that I had laying around, each four feet long and about sixteen inches in diameter. One pipe was heavy-duty plastic, and the other was prefab concrete. Both had been sitting in my pasture for years, left over from a previous owner. We put them vertically in the hole and surrounded them with rocks four feet deep. Those rocks, which were simply sifted from the dirt we had dug from the hole, became the floor of my greenhouse (the floor is four feet below ground).

Special greenhouse timbers, treated with no toxic chemicals, were used to build the four-foot retaining walls and "dead men" anchors. The center was left as a walking path. The planting beds were built at ground level, so that I would not have to stoop to garden, which is one of my favorite parts of my greenhouse. I used recycled steel grates to cover the two open pipes in the floor, so that I didn't step into them on accident and hurt myself. The four-foot-deep planting beds were filled with two feet of excavated soil, topped with a foot of manure and straw and hay, topped with a foot of my homemade compost, topped with a couple of inches of commercial organic compost.

TOMATO TRIAL BY "ICE"

The greenhouse was finished in the first week of February 2011, and I had already started seeds in the house to plant in it. The whole project, including the cost of all materials and the cost of paying the builders, was $6,200—and I still had no evidence it would actually work. Imagine my relief when it not only worked, but worked perfectly. All I can say is that my wife is very patient with me! I'm grateful she has been willing to let me spend not-insignificant sums of our money to try these things. I love you, Charmayne!

Because my greenhouse had no artificial heat at all, I knew that I would need to plant the same winter vegetable varieties in it that I use in the cold frames and hotbeds in the backyard garden. So I had started seeds for kale, winter lettuces, and Swiss chard, and on the day the builders finished my new geothermal greenhouse, I transplanted those into the greenhouse. While they were building (the whole project took three weeks) I had also been doing many hours of research to find out what varieties of tomatoes might survive in a geothermal greenhouse.

I knew tomatoes could grow in winter because an organic CSA owner in Provo had grown winter tomatoes in a greenhouse heated with natural gas. (CSA stands for Community-Supported Agriculture. It means people subscribe to the farm, paying a fee for weekly vegetable deliveries from the farmer). But I needed tomato varieties that could not only survive but thrive in near-freezing nighttime temperatures. I had no idea if such a tomato existed. But I knew that if it did exist, the only place I would be able to find it was among the twelve thousand tomato varieties offered by the backyard gardeners who are members of Seeds Savers Exchange. I poured over the 2010 SSE Yearbook, which lists thousands of vegetable varieties that are not sold by any commercial vendor anywhere. I narrowed my search down to four tomato varieties that seemed most promising: Vee One, Mountain Princess, Snow Fairy, and Silvery Fir Tree. I contacted each of the gardeners who have preserved these extremely rare, cold-tolerant tomato varieties from extinction, and I got seed from each of them.

The results: They all grew!

I'll start with the worst winter performers. The Vee One plants did okay, but struggled when finally planted outside in May. The Silvery Fir Tree tomatoes all died when planted outside in May.

Mountain Princess and Snow Fairy both did great, growing into huge tomato plants. The best part is that the last of these plants are still in my greenhouse today—the same plants—now thirteen months later, still producing fresh tomatoes. They have never been moved, and they have thrived in the greenhouse over two winters and one summer where the temperatures in the greenhouse hit at least 130 degrees—as high as my thermometer goes. But the slight air current from the pipes eight feet deep in the ground, combined with three roof vents that were left open all summer, kept enough air flow that the tomatoes luxuriated in the heat. I have to admit I was shocked. I was sure they would die of heat. But they loved it.

Eventually, in December 2011, most of the original tomato plants had grown so large that they collapsed on themselves. Because I had never imagined them living through the summer heat in the greenhouse, I had never bothered to give them any support. So I cleaned out most of these plants. A couple of the tomato plants, without support, had

125

The Geothermal Winter Greenhouse

decided to grow over the side of the four-foot retaining wall that faced south (where the wall got full sunlight most of the day). These plants were huge and had hundreds of tomatoes on them, so I knew they were enough for my family for the entire winter. But one night in late December, a violent wind storm blew open one of the roof vents that was latched poorly. The low temperature that night was below zero—not just below freezing, but below zero! A couple younger Roma tomato plants—transplanted from the garden in late September—froze to death that night. The top leaves of the year-old tomato plant (which had never been out of the greenhouse) died too. At first, it appeared that the year-old plants would recover. But over the next six weeks, they slowly died. Amazingly, however, the plants still had green tomatoes on them, and those green tomatoes continued to ripen. We continued to eat them until April, and they tasted great! I have long known that one way to preserve autumn tomatoes is to pull up the entire plant before the first freeze and hang it in the garage or cellar, letting the tomatoes slowly ripen on the vine—I have used this method successfully. Apparently the same concept works equally as well on six-foot-long tomato plants that have died by accidental freezing in the winter greenhouse.

It is worth noting that that open vent, which was right above the tomatoes, did not affect any other plant in the greenhouse that night, just the tomatoes. Everything else was unfazed—even the flowers.

FRESH WINTER VEGETABLES

Right after the greenhouse was completed in February 2011, I transplanted green zucchini and yellow squash into the greenhouse, both started from seed in the house in January. Those plants thrived. I hand-pollinated them to harvest squash. (You can find step-by-step instructions for hand-pollinating squash in my first book, *The Forgotten Skills of Self-Sufficiency Used by the Mormon Pioneers.* It only takes a couple minutes.)

Now, thirteen months later, there is not much I have not grown in the greenhouse. On page 128 is a list of what I have grown successfully. Those vegetables eaten directly from the greenhouse are the winter varieties listed in this book. For seed-starting and growing transplants for the summer garden, I have grown the usual summer varieties. At least a couple dozen tomato plants sprouted themselves in the fall, left over from seed from tomatoes that had fallen in the greenhouse during summer. I can't think of any plant that I haven't at least been able to start in the greenhouse for transplant. I did have a couple pole beans freeze in a plastic pot in the greenhouse one January night—they were about two months old. None of the vents had been open. It had been a cold night, but nothing else in the greenhouse was touched.

VENTS

I have three vents in my greenhouse. I leave the vents open twenty-four hours a day from March to November. This is because it is always about thirty degrees warmer in the greenhouse than it is outside. One vent is above the door, and it is closed with a flap made of plywood on hinges. This vent never closes tightly and has never been insulated at all. There is a smaller vent on the opposite wall, which is also closed by a hinged piece of plywood and has never been insulated. The third vent is a double-pane glass window about twenty-four inches by eighteen inches. The first two vents are at the top of the greenhouse, at the highest point of the roof. Having them both open at once creates a cross-current of air. I only open them both in summer. In winter I open only the vent above the door and only during daylight hours. I have left this vent open overnight on accident in December, January, and February with no damage at all inside the greenhouse. But I still try to remember to close it at dusk each night. I should note that there is also a ground-level hole on one wall where the gutter drains the greenhouse roof into barrels. This hole has never been filled. I mention this, and the fact that my vent covers have never covered tightly at all, only to point out that it is not necessary, even on the most bitter winter nights, for my greenhouse to be airtight. Like my cold frames and hotbeds, the greenhouse seems to benefit from some minor, twenty-four-hour-a-day air flow.

GROWN IN THE GREENHOUSE

VEGETABLES

- Carrots
- Tomatoes
  (at least three dozen varieties)
- Swiss chard
- Beets
- Turnips
- Rutabaga
- Kale
- Peas
- Bush beans
- Pole beans
- Lettuce
  (about two dozen varieties)
- Chinese cabbage
- Mustard greens
- Onions
- Leeks
- Cantaloupe
- Watermelon
- Winter squash
- Summer squash

HERBS

- Winter savory
- Sage
- Basil
- Rosemary
- Chives

EXOTICS

- Stevia
- Inca berry
- Acai berry
- Banana palm trees
  (sprouted from seed in January!)
- Pineapple
- Orange tree
- Fig tree

FLOWERS

- Hibiscus
- Christmas cactus
- Zinnias
- Marigolds
- Coleus
- Mums
- Azaleas
  (but they don't like the heat inside the greenhouse come late spring)

WATERING THE GREENHOUSE

In the summer, even when the temperature was 130 degrees, I watered the greenhouse once a week. (If I have plants in pots, instead of in large beds, then the pots dry out faster and have to be watered much more frequently.) In winter, there is no running water to my greenhouse. To solve this problem, I have put a gutter at the bottom of the roofline. The gutter drains into a garden hose, which goes through a wall of the greenhouse and into two fifty-gallon barrels inside the greenhouse. This water has never even come close to freezing, and I use it in fall, winter, and spring to water the greenhouse. I pump the water out of the barrels using a five-dollar plastic hand pump of the kind sold in stores for pumping kerosene. The barrels were given to me for free by a neighbor. I pump water into a five-dollar plastic watering can from the local hardware store and use that to water the plants. In the summer, because we live in a desert, we have outdoor irrigation water that is turned on by the city from May to October. During those months, I can put a garden hose through the greenhouse window to water if there has not been enough rain left in the barrels.

The Geothermal Winter Greenhouse

ANIMALS IN THE WINTER GREENHOUSE

In my research, I have learned that some people who have pit greenhouses keep their chickens and rabbits in them over winter, both to keep the animals warmer and to use the body heat of the animals to help keep the greenhouse warmer at night. I had originally planned to keep my chickens and rabbits in my greenhouse over winter, but I never got around to it. I have kept baby chicks in the greenhouse in early spring, with a light to warm them during the night. (There is no electricity to the greenhouse, so to get a light in there, I had to string a couple heavy-duty extension cords together from the house and put the cord through one of the vents, which never closes with less than a half-inch gap anyway.) I don't see any problem with keeping small animals in the greenhouse over winter. But my greenhouse is small, and I have chosen to use all the space to grow plants rather than giving some of it over to the animals who don't really need it. (My rabbits and chickens are free-range in the winter and do just fine. The chickens sleep in the coop at night, and the rabbits sleep in a tunnel they dug under the hay in the hay room.)

Notes

1. Benson Agriculture and Food Institute, "Walipini Construction," 1.

Caleb Warnock

APHIDS
IN THE WINTER GARDEN

IN COLD FRAMES

I have never had aphid problems in a cold frame. Because cold frames are more exposed to winter chill at night, I don't imagine aphids would ever be a problem in a cold frame. But if you have a problem with them, try one of my solutions below.

IN HOTBEDS

I have only had aphid problems in a winter hotbed once. On one hand, having aphids is actually a good sign—it means the hotbed is certainly warm and working correctly! At first, I ignored the problem, sure they could not survive long. After all, the temperature outside the hotbed was hitting minus seventeen degrees on some nights, even though all the plants in the hotbed were thriving.

But the aphids were thriving too, and they got worse and worse. I consulted some organic gardeners and found a solution that worked really well for me: a sacrificial plant.

It turns out that aphids love some plants more than others, so if you put a plant they *love* in a hotbed with plants they just *like*, they tend to move from like to love. This worked unbelievably well in my hotbed. The aphids never went away, but they were happy to leave the rest of the three-foot by two-foot hotbed mostly alone. They gathered on the sacrificial plant, and we ate everything else.

After a lot of experimenting, I have discovered that aphids love more than anything a variety of Chinese cabbage called "Tai Sai." They literally flock to it. They also love viola flowers, but they tend to kill violas fairly quickly. Tai Sai is hardier against the attack of aphids and can last a couple months in a hotbed as the aphids feed on it, which

•MARCH OF THE APHID INFANTRY•

Once established in a hotbed or garden, aphids can quickly become a major problem because they are smart when it comes to reproduction. Basically, if there is a way to produce babies, aphids use it: They lay eggs. They also use live birth. But worst of all, aphids are almost entirely parthenogenetic. This is the scientific word for having babies without a man. (As a man, I take especial offense to this!) This means that almost all aphids are female only, and they produce babies without ever needing fertilization. The babies are genetic clones. And they do this every twenty days or so. So aphids in the greenhouse or hotbed in winter, when there is a lack of natural predators like ladybugs, can quickly become a problem. The good news is that aphids don't hurt most plants, especially if the plants are established. But they can do a real number on any brassica vegetable—broccoli, cabbage, kale, cauliflower, Chinese cabbages, Brussels sprouts. Left unchecked, aphids will slowly mutilate these vegetables, and they can even kill them.

makes Tai Sai Chinese cabbage my favorite sacrificial plant both for hotbeds and for the greenhouse.

Using sacrificial plants also completely solved my slug problem in the first winter I had my geothermal greenhouse. I grew a beautiful crop of winter lettuce, but the slugs liked the lettuce too. I had already started some Tai Sai in pots in the greenhouse, so I took a couple and set them in among the lettuce plants. Within two days, the slugs had moved to the Tai Sai and for the most part never touched my lettuce again. Sigh of relief. Just another reason I swear by sacrificial plants as organic pest control.

During the summer of 2011, my greenhouse hit between 120 and 130 degrees every day. My tomatoes and kale, surprisingly, loved it. Those same tomatoes and kale are still growing happily in my greenhouse as I write this in February 2012. I only mention this here because I think those hot temperatures killed the slugs—the winter following that hot summer, I never had a single slug in the greenhouse. Not a one.

IN THE GEOTHERMAL GREENHOUSE

The second winter (2011–2012) I had my geothermal greenhouse, I wanted some mature flowers to brighten the greenhouse for the winter and stave off the blues I always feel at the end of the summer garden. Because there is no artificial heat or electricity in my greenhouse, I did some research in two-hundred-year-old gardening books

Aphids in the Winter Garden

to see what would bloom all winter. In October, at my favorite local nursery, I bought violas, Christmas cactus, and mums—all of them were already in flower, which is what I wanted (and the only reason I bought them, rather than growing them myself).

This turned out to be a mistake. What I did not know at the time is that I was bringing aphids into my greenhouse on the violas. By Christmas, my entire greenhouse was terribly infested. I started some Tai Sai from seed, but they were slow to grow, and the aphids were out of control. So I turned to the internet for help.

Using any kind of synthetic chemical was out of the question for me, because I don't want to eat food sprayed with synthetic chemicals, and I was not willing to put any kind of poison in my wholly organic greenhouse. I also didn't want to spend money on chemicals. So I needed a purely organic, no-cost solution. After consulting a lot of organic gardeners on the Internet, I made my own aphid killer. It was simple and free, and it worked extremely well. Here is the recipe:

HOMEMADE, CALEB-TESTED, FREE AND ORGANIC APHID KILLER

- 1 quart water
- 1 garlic bulb (a whole bulb, not a clove)
- 1 large onion
- 1 heaping Tbsp. cayenne pepper

I put a quart of water in a blender. I plopped the entire garlic bulb in and blended it up—no chopping beforehand. Then I put in a large, whole onion from my garage. I used an onion that had begun to go soft, only because I didn't want to use one of the onions I would be eating. I got the cayenne pepper out of my spice cabinet. I blended these until everything was puréed.

As you can imagine, this smells exactly like its ingredients, so I took it out on the back porch and poured it into a glass mason jar, put a tight lid on it, and then brought it back into the house and put it on top of the fridge overnight. I knew it was ready the next day when my wife said to me "Something really stinks over by the fridge." (I never told her what it was. You might want to put your concoction in the garage overnight.) I poured half of the mixture into a second quart jar, so now I had two quart jars, each half full. I added water to both until they were full and left them to sit a second night. In the morning, the vegetable purée had settled into the bottom of the jars. Careful not to disturb the settled stuff, I poured the clear liquid from the top half of the jar into a spray bottle. In the greenhouse, I used all the liquid, spraying everything, being careful to spray the underside of all the leaves. This took about a half hour.

The next day, most of the aphids were dead, but not all. So I took the second jar of my concoction, which had been sitting outside on the back porch overnight, and poured the clear top half into my spray bottle and did the whole thing again.

The next day, every aphid was dead, dead, dead. The greenhouse smelled like garlic for a couple days but not overwhelmingly so. The real problem was that this spray must have been super potent because, to my surprise, it actually killed my seedlings—lettuce, radishes, extra-dwarf pak choi, and even some weed seedlings. Any plant more than a week old was fine and not harmed at all, but those tiny seedlings died as fast as the aphids did. Lucky for me, it was early January and I only had a few baby seedlings anyway. If I need to use this again, I will cover any seedlings before I spray.

This method worked well and actually cured my problem for longer than I expected. The aphids did not return in force until a month later. But this time, instead of spraying again, I decided to try ladybugs. I ordered 1,500 live ladybugs from a company called Hirt's on amazon.com for $8.50. They arrived on February 8, 2012. The kids and I took the ladybugs straight to the greenhouse, and within sixty seconds they were feasting on the aphids—it was really fun to watch. This method solved my problem for the rest of the winter. I did get some aphids on my kale again in summer, but by then I just cut the kale back nearly to the ground and fed the aphid-infested leaves to the cows.

Aphids in the Winter Garden

CALEB'S
WINTER GARDEN JOURNAL

I have kept a garden journal for years because it helps me keep straight when I have planted, what I have planted, when I have harvested, what worked in the garden, and what didn't. More recently, I have begun to blog occasionally about my garden. Below are excerpts from my garden journal from the winter months and a couple of blog entries too. I include some excerpts here because they provide a glimpse of the reality of what my winter garden has looked like through the years.

September 18, 1998

I planted fall crops: radishes, turnips, lettuce, herbs, flowers [my garden journal does not name the varieties, unfortunately].

October 17, 1998

Harvested second crop cabbage.

November 6, 1998

First snowfall; harvested lettuce and radishes

November 21, 1998

I served a homegrown lettuce salad for an early Thanksgiving Dinner. I have been covering the lettuce with blankets to protect it from the snow.

December 3, 2000

Even though the ground is frozen, I planted Japanese Maple tree seeds from the National Arboretum in Washington, DC I planted these using potting soil outside without trays.

October 20, 2007

I got on winter gear and picked apples, four bushels, and put them in the root cellar. The root cellar is stock full. The apples are beautiful and very tasty and crisp and often quite large. We've eaten some vegetables from the root cellar and will continue to eat more. Today I brought in a spaghetti squash and onions.

November 30, 2008

I put seven dozen quarts of apple juice in the freezer today from our trees.

December 21, 2008

We got eleven eggs today.

January 2, 2009

Twelve eggs, a whole dozen. Deep snow and cold.

January 17, 2009

Thirteen eggs—we have eggs coming out our ears. It's bitter cold tonight, in the teens at least.

January 26, 2009

I pulled a spaghetti squash out of the root cellar—got the snow shovel out and dug my way in. It was delicious with my scratch sauce.

February 6, 2009

Fifteen eggs. We are in the eggs now. Fifteen is a lot!

November 2009

The Nov. Brussels sprouts harvested fresh from backyard garden are excellent.

November 16, 2009

It has been two months and ten days since I planted the autumn broccoli and cabbage. They are growing well and are leafy.

November 22, 2009

Today [for a family birthday] we had carrots pulled fresh from under the straw, Brussels sprouts—the last of the year, also fresh from the garden—onions from storage, and beans from the freezer and pumpkin purée from the freezer. I felt very self-sufficient, and of course it all tasted great. I made caramelized carrots, beans, Brussels sprouts and onions. Yum. It snowed about an inch.

November 28, 2009

I built a hoop house. It was kind of a whim. My broccoli and cabbage were getting frost damage. Tonight the hoop house was steamy. On Thanksgiving we had rampicante, carrots, pumpkin, onion, and grape juice from our garden.

February 14, 2010

Planted six broccoli and six cabbage and planted them in a hoop house tunnel, which is still in one piece though one loop did fall, collapsing one end (most have frozen and died by now). We have twelve chickens and get four to eight eggs a day. We've had a wonderful winter out in the garden—we are still taking perfect carrots out of the garden from under a foot of straw. We ate the last rampicante zucchini out of the root cellar this month. The potatoes have stored perfectly in the garage.

September 16, 2010

Cold frame planted: Brown Goldring lettuce, Marvel of Four Seasons lettuce, Tai Sai Chinese cabbage, America spinach, extra dwarf pak choi, Red Russian kale, corn salad, Mache Verte d'Etampes.

October 26, 2010

Woke to first snow on the ground, which melted, and new snow fell this afternoon. I made a winter omelet using Tai Sai out of a balmy cold frame, extra dwarf pak choi from garden bed, Swiss chard, onion, medium winter carrot finely shredded, mozzarella cheese, salt and pepper—excellent taste.

October 27, 2010

We got four inches of snow at our house last night, and I'm pleased to report that this morning my winter lettuce is not frozen, not dead, but is in fact as happy as a clam. Good eating this winter! And I mean for our family, not for the deer—I've put inexpensive fencing around the lettuce patch. I've learned the hard way that deer are also big fans of fresh winter lettuce!

Interestingly, the colder it has gotten, the more beautiful the colors have gotten in the lettuce too. And the tender varieties in the hotbed are thriving too. This morning I used a soil thermometer to measure the heat (the cold frame is compost-heated three feet underground, using chicken manure compost).

THE RESULTS

Temp inside the hotbed, six inches deep in soil: a balmy forty-six degrees.

Temp outside the hotbed, six inches deep in soil: a chilly thirty-six degrees.

Ambient air temp outside the cold frame: forty-eight degrees.

So the hotbed, naturally heated, is working exactly as it should. No electricity, and much warmer than the surrounding land. Now that is smart, self-sufficient winter gardening!

November 10, 2010

Omelet bar for dinner with our eggs, onion, spinach, Swiss chard, Tai Sai, and grated carrots, all from the garden. Yum.

November 25, 2010

Last night was seven degrees below zero. I'm pleased to say the hotbeds are doing excellently, kept warm with the compost heating—no losses at all. In the garden I did lose some winter lettuce on the south side, which was most exposed to direct snow. Everything protected by glass over straw bales is doing great.

December 12, 2010

Some of both of the Four Seasons and winter romaine that appeared dead and frozen solid have grown new leaves. I harvested a handful today, enough to have tacos for dinner tonight. This is from the bed only covered by glass. For the most part the lettuce is doing fine. We are getting two to four eggs a day from nine chickens.

December 26, 2010

We bought two heads of romaine lettuce from the grocery store. We need a lot more compost-heated winter lettuce. I've used it a lot. Tai Sai is infested with aphids.

January 2, 2011

It was minus four at 9:45 last night—frigid. Probably got to minus fifteen. Winter lettuces have sprouted in the house. I built a wooden cold frame this week.

January 16, 2011

I put about two dozen winter lettuces into two new hotbeds installed in the backyard garden. We've had three nights of minus fifteen degrees. Not quite that cold since I planted the lettuce, which is all doing well. Even the unprotected lettuces, spinach, and Swiss chard are popping out new leaves again.

January 17, 2011 (blog entry at caleb-warnock.blogspot.com)

There are at least three inches of snow on the ground. Over the past three weeks we have had three nights at our house that reached minus fifteen degrees—you read that right. And I'm having garden-fresh salad. Great to be me!

But how much did that salad cost you, you may be asking? After all, the price of the greenhouse, the electricity, the artificial heat, the artificial lighting . . . that's an expensive salad.

So wrong.

First, you should know this salad was picked within the hour, photographed, and eaten. There is no greenhouse. No cold frame, no hotbed, no artificial heating of any kind, no artificial lighting, no special glass growing frame, no electricity, not a single thing that costs money or requires work. Not a single thing.

I have not been out digging, nor planting, nor doing anything special to get this salad. Just five minutes of work last September and a little planning. That's all.

And now, on January 16th, with temperatures hovering at freezing, I have fresh winter salad. Even better, I have enough for tomorrow, and the next day, and the next, and on and on. I could even make a fresh winter salad for a crowd.

Zero cost. Zero special nonsense. Just forgotten skills of self-sufficiency of the pioneers.

February 17, 2011

Last night at 1 a.m. the soil temperature in the greenhouse was forty-one and forty-three degrees in various spots six inches deep, and outside, the ground was frozen so solid I couldn't get the thermometer in!

February 27, 2011

Xander and I planted the vegetable starts in the greenhouse: zucchini, kale, Swiss chard, and tomatoes. It snowed most of the day and the greenhouse was seventy degrees. Yesterday evening at 8:30 p.m. it was forty-three degrees in the greenhouse (air) and thirty-three degrees outside. In the greenhouse, the zucchini is up; Snow Fairy tomatoes, kale, Swiss chard, onion growing green threads. At 10:30 p.m. it was forty-five degrees inside the greenhouse and thirty degrees outside; stormy and two inches of snow.

October 29, 2011 (blog entry at caleb-warnock.blogspot.com)

I continue to be asked this question: Do you *really* eat self-sufficiently?

It's a fair question—after all, I wrote the book on it. *The Forgotten Skills of Self-Sufficiency Used by the Mormon Pioneers* is not a research-based book. This is how we live. We eat out off our two acres every day of the year, no matter the season. It's not hard, it's not time consuming, it certainly saves us huge amounts of money (I'll be happy to compare my monthly or yearly grocery store bill to anyone's—I'll win, I promise).

Someone asked me to tour their garden recently and give them some advice.

While they were showing me their spread, this person said to me, "It must be nice to stay home all day gardening and researching for your next book."

Um, so wrong. I have a full-time job (journalist for the *Provo Daily Herald*) and several part-time jobs (teaching writing classes both in person and online, book tour and book writing, directing writing conferences, selling pure, non-hybrid seed raised on our own property, teaching gardening and homemade yeast and self-sufficiency classes). I'm one of the few lucky people who not only gets to do exactly what I love every day (garden, write, teach), but I am also over-employed in an under-employed economy. (Don't mistake that for well-paid. If you knew what writers get paid, you'd weep. There is a reason we are self-sufficient.)

So no, I don't have luxuriant free time to lounge around gardening and cooking and researching books. This is just our life. I was paid one of the highest compliments of my life this week when a friend looked at me and said "You are the epitome of 'If you need something done, ask a busy person.'" Made my day.

I say all of this because everyone can do something to feed themselves, no matter your schedule or where you live—a huge farm, a couple of acres, a condo, a rented apartment. I have lived in all of these, and I have grown my own food on all of these properties to some degree. If you want to do it, you can.

So, to answer the question "Do you *really* eat self-sufficiently?" I'm going to try to blog more often about what we are eating, to show you. And I'll try to take some pictures, if I can remember. (It's hard for a hungry person to remember to stop and take a photo.) Here is some of what we ate this week:

PASTA SAUCE

This is what I made today. In this dish from our garden: onion, carrot, beet, tomatoes, basil, Japanese purple mustard, Swiss chard. I diced the onions, removed the stems from the mustards and chard, grated the carrot and beet, and put the tomatoes whole, with all the rest, into the blender with salt for a few minutes and then put the purée on the stove on the lowest possible heat for about an hour and a half. We are actually eating this tomorrow for Sunday dinner over whole wheat pasta, so the sauce is in the fridge as we "speak."

PIZZA

In this dish from our property: dough made from homemade, natural yeast, sauce made from our tomatoes, and basil (puréed and simmered for an hour with salt; I should have put in one of our onions, but I forgot). Also worth mentioning—artisan cheese made locally at Heber Valley Artisan Cheese, which I love!

CREAM STEW

In this stew from our garden: purple podded pole beans (dried, grown from our own seed); contender beans (dried); white, yellow, orange, and red carrots; turnip; corn.

GARDEN SALAD

In this salad from our garden: a gourmet lettuce blend of Rouge Grenobloise (a red lettuce), Green Jewel romaine (grown from our own seed), oak leaf lettuce (light green and frilly), Merveille de Quatre Saison (bronze and green lettuce); also, orange and yellow carrots.

TOAST AND EGGS

In this dish from our property: fresh eggs, toast from homemade bread made with homemade natural yeast. (Raw honey from my parents' farm—that deserves a mention).

GARDEN SOUP

In this soup from our garden: potatoes (grown from our own seed potatoes), rutabaga, Swiss chard, onion, basil, carrots, tomatoes (puréed fresh). Also in this soup: lentils, chickpeas, brown rice, hamburger. No recipe. All garden soups are the same—fill the pot about two-thirds with water, bring to boil, put in veggies, cook, season to taste. I added the chard at the last minute.

TOAST

(Several times this week—it's been toast weather). Using homemade bread baked with homemade, natural yeast, spread with an assortment of our homemade jams and jellies.

SANDWICHES

Using homemade bread baked with homemade, natural yeast, and lettuces from the garden.

OMELETS

The kids have been demanding these, especially Xander. Made with our fresh, free-range eggs, of course.

APPLES

We have apples coming out our ears. I've given dozens away this week, and the kids gobble them up off the trees, and Charmayne makes wonderful apple crisp, and tomorrow for a treat we are having gjetost cheese over apple slices broiled for two minutes—a new favorite treat that a friend introduced me to today. The broiled cheese tastes exactly like caramel on the apples. So good!

Do we go to the grocery store? And for what? Yes, of course we do. I like to tell people that I'm retired from milking cows—after growing up with a milk cow. All that fresh milk and cream is great. What is not great is having to milk the cow twice a day whether it is 120 degrees or minus 20 degrees. And you can't go on vacation. And milk cows are the orneriest creatures on earth. On many occasions in my youth, I would milk the cow in the dark during a blizzard (and mind you we had no milking barn; I had to milk out in the weather), and just before I'd finish, the cow would kick over the milk bucket. A couple of times when this happened, I'm not ashamed to say I literally cried. A couple other times I had some choice words for the cow. So we don't have a milk cow, and we go to the grocery store for milk, cream, yogurt, and cheese—and

I'm happy to do it. My goal in life is to continue being "retired" from milking cows.

We also buy wheat in bulk for grinding our own flour, and we buy some meat. We don't really eat processed food—no soda at our house, and chips only rarely. We buy pasta. Oranges and bananas. We buy oats in five-gallon buckets. I buy chocolate chips to make cookies with. We've pretty well weaned ourselves off of cold cereal. One day I came to the realization that cold cereal was getting more and more expensive and the boxes were getting smaller and lighter. So I have pretty much stopped eating it completely. My wife still has cereal sometimes.

November 3, 2011

Planted hotbeds today: peas, Grand Rapids lettuce, Winter Green Jewel romaine.

November 9, 2011

Lettuce has sprouted in the hotbed.

Thanksgiving Day 2011

The peas in the north cold frame came up today. I noticed this when I transplanted strawberries into the frame. I also put cold frames over the Swiss chard and cabbage today. Quite cold lately, nearing single digits at night.

144

Caleb Warnock

I transplanted America spinach into a cloche that I bought at auction last week. Put glass house over the lettuce. The pole beans and lettuce in the greenhouse are doing great.

November 26, 2011

Planted watermelon radishes in the greenhouse.

December 1, 2011

I closed up the cold frames for the cabbages and Swiss chard with soil around the edges. The next couple of days will be the first continuous forty-eight hours below freezing. Peas, cabbage, chard, lettuces, mangel beets, onions, mustard all doing well. More peas up today in second hotbed. The greenhouse was 108 degrees without vents open today at 3 p.m. 78 degrees with vents at sundown; outside temp was 38.

December 25, 2011

For Christmas dinner we ate fresh: three gallons of grape juice, eggs and onions in breakfast quiche, pumpkin pie from garage, yeast bread, lettuce blend of tennis ball, romaine, Winter Density, with Swiss chard and turnip greens. Fresh outside is extra dwarf pak choi, mangel, lettuce hard, rutabaga, mustard greens, beets, carrots, turnips (purple and Boule d'Or varieties), spinach, thyme, oregano.

Fresh in the greenhouse: tomatoes, pak choi, stevia

Fresh in the frames outside: lettuce, peas, strawberry plants

Cellared in the garage: pumpkins, onions, rampicante zucchini, tomatoes

December 26, 2011

I watered all the cold frames (by hand) today at 3 p.m. with temps at thirty-eight degrees.

January 1, 2012

Eighty degrees in the greenhouse at 4:30 today with the vent open all day. Five eggs today, seven yesterday. Forty-two degrees outside today; never any snow this winter; strangely warm, but it has been a great winter garden so far. I made tomato-chickpea-lime soup with pumpkin, onions, and carrots from the garden and a quart and a half of frozen summer tomatoes with top stem cut out. Yesterday I took eight fresh tomatoes from the greenhouse to a New Year's Eve party.

January 2, 2012 (blog entry at calebwarnock.blogspot.com)

The winter garden is thriving. . . . We've been eating a lot out of the garden lately, which is really fun in the winter. We went to the grocery store tonight and bought some yogurt and a few cheapo, too-ripe bananas for the kids. Don't need to buy tomatoes—we have those in abundance. (Yes, in January. And yes, I just used a quart and a half of them to make the best tomato-lime-chickpea soup) No need to buy lettuce, or potatoes, or onions, or squash, or any greens—we have all that. Certainly don't need to buy eggs—we got five more of those from the chickens just today alone. Fresh carrots? Got those. Turnips? Check. Rutabaga? Check. I don't have fresh peas right now, only because I didn't plan very well. But the peas are up. The last ones sprouted in the cold frame on Christmas Day. We even have pole beans (in the green house).

By the way, it's been in the 80s every day in the greenhouse, and that's with the vents open all day.

In the backyard, the baby lettuce in the hotbed is thriving. The Swiss chard is happy as a clam in the cold frame. All ten of my experimental winter lettuces are doing well with absolutely no protection. I am testing these ten varieties of winter lettuce as a volunteer researcher for the federal government. There is a clear winner, which I won't announce for now, since the seed is not available for purchase anywhere. I'm proud to say that I will be the first person in the world to offer this seed for sale, because I'm the only garden researcher working with the federal seed bank to test winter lettuces! I'm enjoying it a lot.

January 3, 2012

Today in the greenhouse I planted Noir des Carmes in direct soil with Minnesota Midget cantaloupe, Tai Sai, Giant Swiss pansies, and banana tree seeds. It was fifty degrees outside today, worryingly warm. It was one hundred degrees in the greenhouse with one vent open, eighty degrees when I opened all the vents.

January 13, 2012

Tai Sai sprouted today in the greenhouse. Temp inside greenhouse at dusk was 80 degrees with the large vent open all day. Yesterday we got two Holstein steers (cattle for the pasture).

January 15, 2012

Planted Tom Thumb peas in the greenhouse today.

January 18, 2012

Dug a new hotbed yesterday and another one today. I built a hotbed lid today and planted seed directly into hotbed soil—Red Iceberg lettuce, Rose orach [a spinach-like vegetable], winter savory, collard vates, Yugoslavian red butterhead, Osaka Purple mustard greens, bountiful bush bean, Tom Thumb pea, Yellow Spanish globe onion, Erlyn Madsen cucumber.

January 29, 2012

The greenhouse was sixty-eight degrees at 4:30 with the vent open all day, and the soil temperature at six inches deep was forty-eight degrees, amazingly. The Tom Thumb peas have been coming up over the past three days.

February 8, 2012

It's official: I have sprouted a second banana tree. It had sprouted its first leaf a couple weeks ago, but because it was a cotyledon and not a "true" leaf [a "cotyledon" is the scientific term for the embryonic first leaf that comes out of a seed. In some cases, the cotyledon does not at all resemble the "true" leaves that come out next. True leaves look like what the actual plant will look like.], it was impossible to tell for sure whether it was really a banana tree or just some errant weed. Well, this morning when I went out to feed the chickens, this second banana tree had sprouted its first two tiny, true, palm-like leaves overnight, proving beyond a doubt that I now have sprouted two January-planted banana trees in my geothermal greenhouse in Utah in winter! That is the most exciting accomplishment yet in my winter garden—especially because the seed package said those seeds would take "between 2–26 weeks to germinate" and "only germinates at temperatures 75 degrees and above." So sprouting not one but two is exciting! Even Charmayne is impressed—and it's hard to impress my wife.

147

BIBLIOGRAPHY

1897 Sears Roebuck & Co. Catalogue. Sears, Roebuck & Company, 1897. Facsimile of the first edition, with an introduction by Nick Lyons. New York: Skyhorse Publishing, 2007.

"About Us." Seed Savers Exchange. Accessed Aug. 3, 2010. http://www.seedsavers.org.

Albert, Steve. "Winter or Late-Season Apple Varieties." *Harvest to Table* (blog). Dec. 29, 2006. Accessed Jul. 12, 2012. http://harvesttotable.com/2006/12/winter_apple_varieties/.

American Livestock Breeds Conservancy. "Rare Breed Facts—Why Raise Rare Breeds?" Accessed Sept. 7, 2012. http://albc-usa.org/EducationalResources/rarebreedfacts.html.

Benson Agriculture and Food Institute. "Walipini Construction (The Underground Greenhouse)." Brigham Young University. Revised version, 2002. Accessed Jul. 12, 2012. http://bensoninstitute.org/Publication/Manuals/Walipini.pdf.

Center for Biodiversity and Conservation. "Biodiversity and Your Food: Did You Know?" American Museum of Natural History. Accessed Jun. 6, 2012. http://www.amnh.org/our-research/center-for-biodiversity-conservation/publications/general-interest/living-with-biodiversity-series.

Centers for Disease Control and Prevention. "Multistate Outbreak of Listeriosis Linked to Whole Cantaloupes from Jensen Farms, Colorado." Last modified Dec. 8, 2011. Accessed Jul. 9, 2012. http://www.cdc.gov/listeria/outbreaks/cantaloupes-jensen-farms/index.html.

Close, C. P. "Bulletin No. 76 - Forcing Lettuce." *UAES Bulletins,* Mar. 1, 1902, Paper 98. Accessed Jul. 12, 2012. http://digitalcommons.usu.edu/uaes_bulletins/98.

Cornell University. "Chlorpropham." Accessed Jul. 9, 2012. http://pmep.cce.cornell.edu/profiles/extoxnet/carbaryl-dicrotophos/chlorpropham-ext.html.

"Couer De Boeuf Des Vertus Cabbage." Baker Creek Heirloom Seed Co. Accessed Jul. 19, 2012. http://rareseeds.com/couer-de-boeuf-des-vertus-cabbage.html.

Dickson, James S. "Radiation Meets Food." *Physics Today*, 65, no. 2 (Feb. 2012). Accessed via PhysicsToday.org on Jul. 9, 2012.

"Early Jersey Wakefield." Baker Creek Heirloom Seed Co. Accessed Jul. 19, 2012. http://rare-seeds.com/early-jersey-wakefield-1-oz.html.

"Fallawater apple." Orange Pippin Ltd. Last modified Jul. 4, 2011. Accessed Jul. 12, 2012. http://www.orangepippin.com/apples/fallawater.

"Food Price Watch—January 2012." The World Bank. Accessed Jul. 13, 2012. http://siteresourc-es.worldbank.org/EXTPOVERTY/Resources/336991-1311966520397/FoodPriceWatchJanu-ary2012.htm.

"Geante Blanche Beet." Baker Creek Heirloom Seed Co. Accessed Jul. 12, 2012. http://rareseeds.com/geante-blanche-beet.html.

"Giant Yellow Eckendorf Beet." Baker Creek Heirloom Seed Co. Accessed Jul. 12, 2012. http://rareseeds.com/vegetablesa-c/beetroot/giant-yellow-eckendorf-beet.html.

"Golden Acre Cabbage." Pinetree Garden Seeds. Accessed Jul. 25, 2012. https://www.superseeds.com/details.php?id=63.

Henderson, Peter. *Henderson's Handbook of Plants and General Horticulture*. New York: Peter Henderson & Company, 1910. Accessed via Archive.org on Jul. 12, 2012.

Isidore, Chris. "How the Floods Will Hurt the Economy." CNNMoney.com, June 16, 2008. Accessed Jul. 9, 2012. http://money.cnn.com/2008/06/16/news/economy/flooding_impact/index.htm.

"Keepsake apple." Orange Pippin Ltd. Last modified Feb. 20, 2012. Accessed Jun. 4, 2012. http://www.orangepippin.com/apples/keepsake.

Keillor, Garrison. "RCA script." Recorded Dec. 31, 2005. Transcript and audio. Accessed Jul. 12, 2012. http://prairiehome.publicradio.org/programs/2005/12/31/scripts/rca.shtml.

Loudon, John Claudius. *An Encyclopedia of Agriculture.* Second Edition. London: Longman, Rees, Orme, Brown, and Green, 1831. Accessed via Google Books on Jul. 12, 2012.

"Mammoth Red Mangel Beet." Baker Creek Heirloom Seed Co. Accessed Jul. 12, 2012. http://rareseeds.com/mammoth-red-mangel-beet.html.

Pliny the Elder. *The Natural History of Pliny.* Vol. 4. Translated by John Bostock and H. T. Riley. London: George Bell & Sons, 1890. Accessed via Google Books on Jul. 9, 2012.

"Tete Noire Cabbage." Baker Creek Heirloom Seed Co. Accessed Jul. 19, 2012. http://rareseeds.com/tete-noire-cabbage.html.

Vilmorin-Andrieux, MM. *The Vegetable Garden: Illustrations, Descriptions, and Culture of the Garden Vegetables of Cold and Temperate Climates.* English edition, third edition. New York: E. P. Dutton and Co., 1920. Accessed via Archive.org on Jul. 12, 2012.

Weathers, John. *French Market-Gardening: Including Practical Details of "Intensive Cultivation" for English Growers.* London: J. Murray, 1909. Accessed via Archive.org on Jul. 9, 2012.

Wild Garden Seed. "Joan." Gathering Together Farm, Inc. Accessed Jul. 12, 2012. http://www.wildgardenseed.com/product_info.php?products_id=182.

"Winter Apples." *Portland Guardian*, Jun. 26, 1895. http://nla.gov.au/nla.news-article65400804.

"Yellow Cylindrical Beet." Baker Creek Heirloom Seed Co. Accessed Jul. 12, 2012. http://rareseeds.com/vegetablesa-c/beetroot/yellow-cylindrical-beet.html.

Bibliography

INDEX

151

153

Index

ABOUT THE AUTHOR

Caleb Warnock

Caleb Warnock was raised in the kitchens and gardens of the last generation to provide family meals without relying on the grocery store. He has won more than a dozen awards for journalism and literature, including the Utah Arts Council Original Writing Contest and the David O. McKay Essay Contest. His writing ranges from articles on wolf-watching in Yellowstone to backyard poultry-keeping to perennial gardening. He has taught writing for the past decade.

Caleb teaches "Forgotten Skills" classes on winter gardening, pioneer jams and jellies, growing early and long-keeper vegetables, raising chickens, and much more.

To reach the author:

Visit CalebWarnock.blogspot.com or e-mail calebwarnock@yahoo.com

TROUBLE'S ON THE MENU

CALEB WARNOCK & BETSY SCHOW

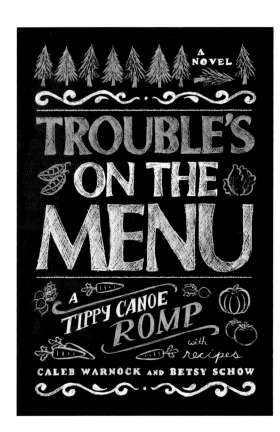

HALLIE DOESN'T BELONG in Barefoot, Montana. She's a California girl used to sunshine and warmth—not cold and snow. But after the unexpected death of her estranged husband, she braves the winter weather to wrap up some of his estate details, only to discover that she doesn't fit in and none of the townspeople like her.

THAT IS, except for the town's handsome mayor, who takes quite an interest in Hallie.

BUT WHEN HIS LIFE starts to spiral out of control, she must decide if he's worth sticking around for in the long term. Join Hallie in this fast-paced, hilarious romance as she learns that sometimes love is the only remedy for a broken heart.

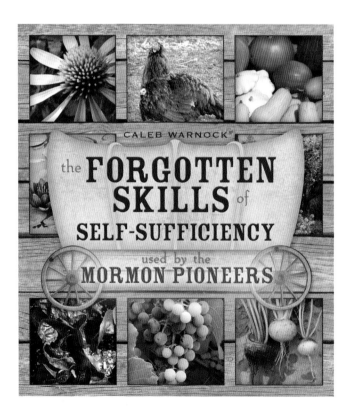

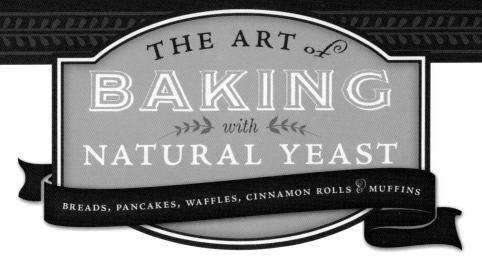

THE ART of BAKING with NATURAL YEAST

BREADS, PANCAKES, WAFFLES, CINNAMON ROLLS & MUFFINS

CALEB WARNOCK & MELISSA RICHARDSON

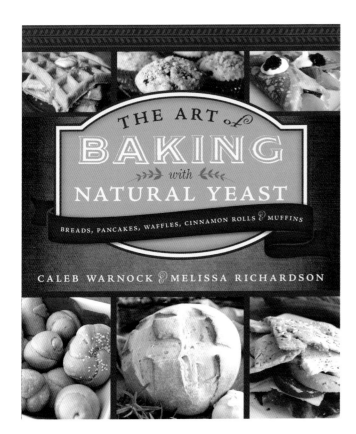

This is the book you've been waiting for! With groundbreaking information about the health benefits of natural yeast, this book will revolutionize the way you bake! Easy to prepare and use, natural yeast breaks down harmful enzymes in grains, makes vitamins and minerals more easily available for digestion, and converts dough into a nutritious food source that won't spike your body's defenses. Improve your digestive health and happiness with these delicious recipes you can't find anywhere else!

BE SURE TO TRY THE:

BLUEBERRY CREAM MUFFINS

QUICK AND EASY CREPES

GARLIC ROSEMARY SOURDOUGH

WHIMSY ROLLS

NO KNEAD BREAD

From quick and easy treats for a busy day to elaborate creations for special events, you'll find something tasty and nutritious to tempt everyone's taste buds!